D1213867

MOHAMMEDANISM

IS VOLUME

143

OF THE

Twentieth Century Encyclopedia of Catholicism

UNDER SECTION

XV

NON-CHRISTIAN BELIEFS

IT IS ALSO THE

68TH

VOLUME IN ORDER OF PUBLICATION

Edited by HENRI DANIEL-ROPS of the Académie Française

MOHAMMEDANISM

By LOUIS GARDET

Translated from the French by WILLIAM BURRIDGE, W. F.

HAWTHORN BOOKS · PUBLISHERS · *New York*

 This book was manufactured in the United States of America and published simultaneously in Canada by McClelland & Stewart, Ltd., 25 Hollinger Road, Toronto 16. It was originally published in France under the title *Connaître l'Islam*. © Librairie Arthème Fayard, 1958. The Library of Congress has catalogued The Twentieth Century Encyclopedia of Catholicism under card number 58-14327. Library of Congress Catalogue Card Number for this volume: 61-8389. The Catholic University of America Library has catalogued this volume based on the Lynn-Peterson Alternative Classification for Catholic Books: BQT184T9v.143/BP161. Suggested decimal classification: 297.

First Edition, June, 1961

NIHIL OBSTAT

Daniel Duivesteijn, S.T.D.

Censor Deputatus

IMPRIMATUR

E. Morrogh Bernard

Vicarius Generalis

Westmonasterii, die IV APRILIS MCMLXI

The Nihil obstat and Imprimatur are a declaration that a book or pamphlet is considered to be free from doctrinal or moral error. It is not implied that those who have granted the Nihil obstat and Imprimatur agree with the contents, opinions or statements expressed.

CONTENTS

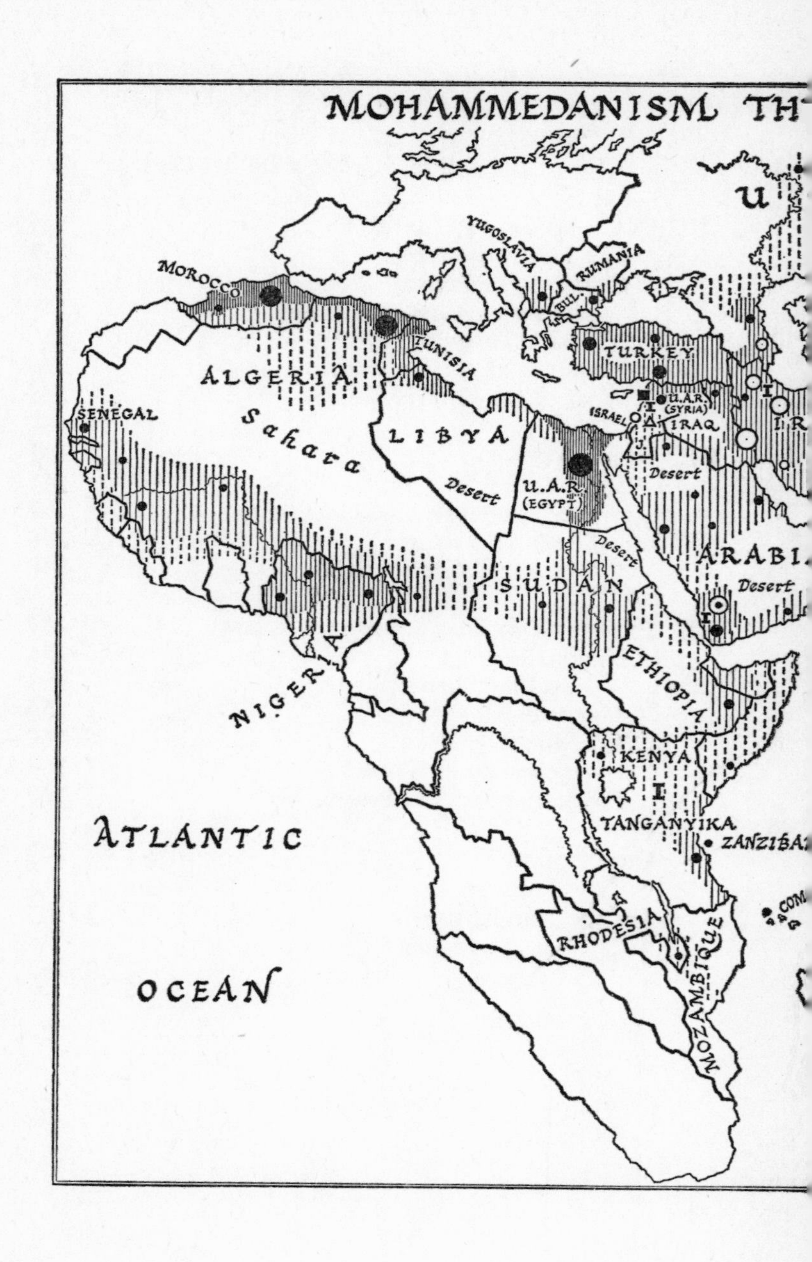
MOHAMMEDANISM TH
MOROCCO
ALGERIA
TUNISIA
Sahara
LIBYA
Desert
U.A.R. (EGYPT)
SENEGAL
NIGERIA
SUDAN
ETHIOPIA
KENYA
TANGANYIKA
ZANZIBA
RHODESIA
MOZAMBIQUE
YUGOSLAVIA
RUMANIA
BUL.
TURKEY
U.A.R. (SYRIA)
ISRAEL
IRAQ
J.
Desert
ARABI
Desert
ATLANTIC
OCEAN

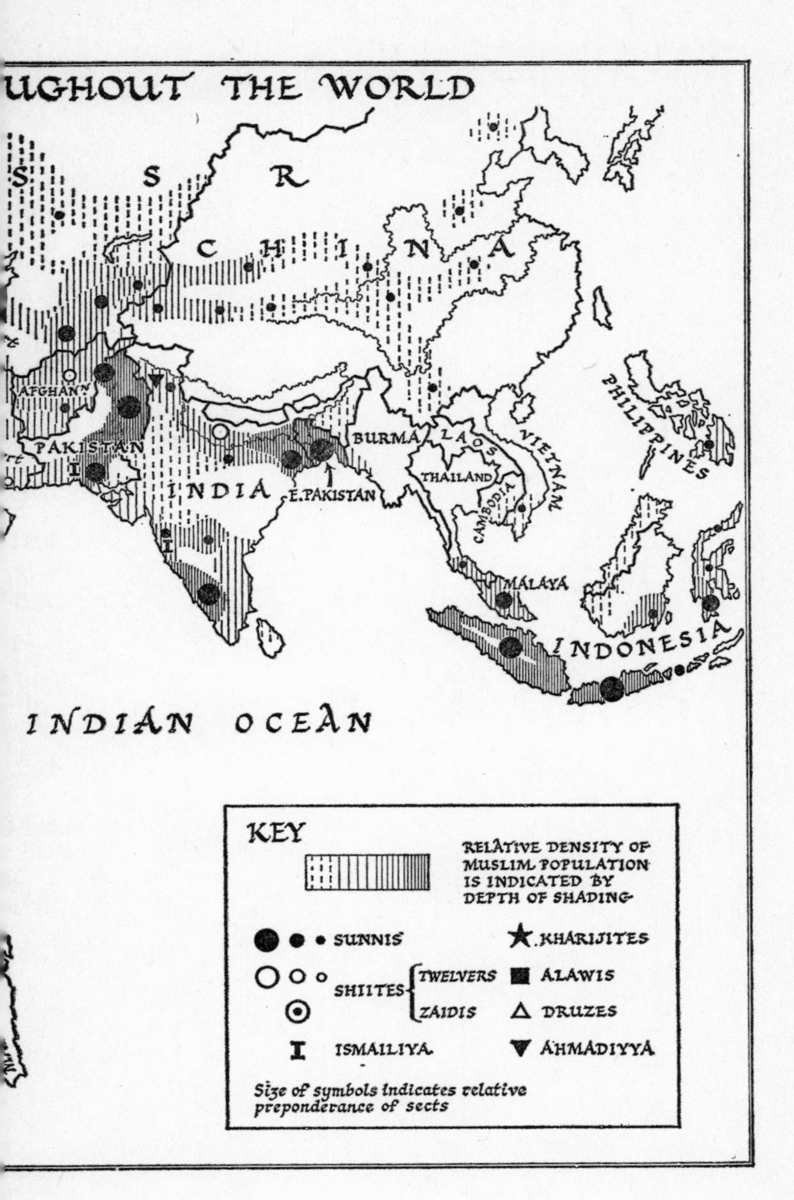
UGHOUT THE WORLD
S S R
CHINA
AFGHAN
PAKISTAN
INDIA
E. PAKISTAN
BURMA
LAOS
THAILAND
CAMBODIA
VIETNAM
PHILIPPINES
MALAYA
INDONESIA
INDIAN OCEAN
KEY
RELATIVE DENSITY OF MUSLIM POPULATION IS INDICATED BY DEPTH OF SHADING
SUNNIS
SHIITES
TWELVERS
ZAIDIS
ISMAILIYA
KHARIJITES
ALAWIS
DRUZES
AHMADIYYA
Size of symbols indicates relative preponderance of sects

MOHAMMEDANISM

INTRODUCTION

Increasingly Islam is making itself felt throughout the world. From Indonesia a great arc stretches almost continuously to Senegal. It has been called the "Crescent of Islam". This vast expanse includes peoples of many races and tongues, with a greatly varied rôle in the history of the world. But whatever their divergences, they profess, each and all, to be fundamentally united in a religious faith from which there springs a common attitude towards the world and mankind. *Ana Muslim*, "I am a Muslim", that can be heard from the lips of people from Pakistan, Somaliland or the Maghreb. And they would still say it even though they no longer had in their religion what a Christian would call a living faith, and were left with only their particular attitude towards the world and mankind. A few figures will help.[1] Statistics vary from author to author: some Western writers tend to minimize them, whereas in books of Arabic origin the inclination may be to set them as high as possible. A total of between 365 million and 400 million seems a fair assessment. One fact must be pointed out. It may be thought that the Arabs and Arabized peoples constitute the largest compact ethnical and linguistic group of Muslims. In reality Pakistan (sixty-six million) and India (forty million), with Urdu, Hindustani and Bengali as their principal languages, together come at the head of the list. Then there is Malaysia (seventy-five to eighty million) and the Turks (sixty million), though two-thirds of them live in the Marxist world. Taken numerically, the Arab and Arabized group comes fourth (sixty million), almost on a level with Iran and the "Iranized" peoples on one hand and the Muslims of "black" Africa on the other. Of these sixty million, two-thirds must

[1] A more complete survey of world statistics will be found in Chapter VII.

be reckoned as Arabized—though they proudly proclaim their incorporation in the Arab peoples of the world.

Statistics, indeed, do not afford an accurate criterion of the importance of these various groups. But three lessons can be learnt from the diversity of peoples belonging to Islam: first the picture of Islam is that of a universalism offering itself to all men of all races. Second, for all that, it is the Arabs and Arabized peoples who throughout the history of Islam, and even today, play the foremost part, so much so that people in the West who are not acquainted with Islam identify, practically speaking, Muslim with Arab. Third, groups of such numbers and cultural wealth as Pakistan and India, Malaya and Indonesia, seem bound to play an important rôle in any future developments, especially now that they are independent countries.

It will help the reader of this book if he keeps these few brief statements in mind. In this book an attempt is made to understand Islam from the inside. It is no easy task and will necessarily entail careful analysis. Ever since last century many specialists have been at work tabulating the religious, cultural and historical content of Islam. Most of them have contributed to an objective approach to the subject and some, by no means the least among them, have created an enlightened and sympathetic atmosphere which is very necessary in any attempt to grasp a mentality so different from our own.

But it is time that a more general public was familiar with the studies that have been done. We dare to hope that the encounter of Islam and the West may lead to friendly relations between Christians and Muslims: and that, we believe, is the wish of many sincere Muslims also, though such a purpose, of course, is too ambitious for these pages. At least we may be able to prepare the way, for when you get to know a man you are on your way to intelligent conversation with him.

In conducting this inquiry, we do not take our stand

primarily on Christian theology. We shall try to see Islam as a Muslim sees it. But, of course, as Christians writing for Christians, we shall frequently refer to Christian concepts in order to keep our statements in perspective. The reader, whether Muslim or Christian, will soon see that that is the only way to begin to get a clear picture of Islam itself: a much more promising method, indeed, than starting off, as has often been done, with one or two focal points drawn solely from the modern, dechristianized West.

The aim of this little work will be achieved if it entices the reader to study the matter more exhaustively and explore for himself the avenues of thought here outlined.

CHAPTER I

THE ORIGINS OF ISLAM

THE PRE-ISLAM SITUATION: SIXTH AND SEVENTH CENTURIES A.D.

The Merovingians, allies of the Empire, strove in vain to halt the Lombard invaders. Italy was devastated. The Emperors Maurice, Phocas and Herculius successively ruled in Byzantium. The last of the Sassanian Kings, Chosroes II, reigned over Iran (Persia).

Between Byzantium and Iran lay the Arabian Peninsula, separated from Abyssinia on the west by a narrow stretch of sea. Its life was in the deserts and the wandering tribes, and, above all, in the trading towns situated at the crossing of the great caravan routes. Its Arab population was of Semitic stock or of peoples assimilated to it. The Yemen, once governed by an Abyssinian viceroy, was, by the end of the sixth century, occupied by the Persians. Jacobites in schism with Rome had installed themselves in the north of the peninsula. Outstanding among them were the Lakhmids, allied to the Persians, and the Ghasanids, who were under the sway of Byzantium. Najran, in the south, was Nestorian.

Then there were the Jewish or Judaized tribes, like the Himyarite king who persecuted his Christian subjects in the fifth century, or the farming and trading tribes of Khaibar and Yathrib, both of them to achieve fame through the pages of the Koran, or again, the Hanifs, who were neither Christian nor Jewish, yet held a monotheism deriving from Abraham.

Most of the Arab tribes, however, were still idolaters. They acknowledged a supreme being, *the* God (*al-ilah*) but indulged also in a polytheism to which each tribe contributed its deities.

The commercial capital was Mecca and there, too, stood the ancient Semitic temple called the Kaaba (the cube), where the black stone from heaven was enshrined and where the pantheism of tribal deities had been assembled with its emblematic statues including a "virgin and child".

The divinity honoured by the southern tribes was called al-Rahman, the Merciful One. The word seems to have been their personal name of God and Islam was later to use it with particular reverence.

It was not unusual to find foreigners, particularly Abyssinian Christians, staying or settling in Mecca. The Kaaba was the cultural and religious rallying point. The annual fair held there included a great competitive festival of poetry. The winning entries, epics, elegies and romantic poems, were carefully lettered out on strips of precious cloth and draped along the walls of the temple. Hither, also, came the tribal pilgrims, for it was here that at dates determined by the lunar calendar ancient rites, undoubtedly symbolical in character, were performed.

The country was organized on the lines of what one may call an aristocratic democracy. It was the chief man of the tribe, at one and the same time "the ancient" (*shaykh*) and the judge (*hakim*), who ruled, accompanied by his notables, In Christian tribes it was often the bishop's task to settle litigations and pronounce and promulgate decisions.

Opposition of one tribe or clan to another was often violent. No less fervid was the sense of tribal unity that did duty for patriotism. Rooted in ties of blood and bonded by sentiments of solidarity, it held together a collection of gigantic families, amongst whom polygamy was allowed, repudiation of wives frequent and the birth of a son looked on as an honour for the family, while often, especially in times of famine when living conditions were particularly hard, an "extra" daughter would be killed at birth or abandoned. For all that, the Arab woman was held in honour for her motherhood. Through her influence over her husband, and still more over her sons, and often, also, by virtue of a social function which was her right, she played a far from negligible rôle in the life of tribe and clan.

The sense of patriarchal and tribal honour reached remarkable heights.[1] Hospitality and mutual aid were sacred; they were virtues ingrained by the constant dangers of nomadic life. Once mutual protection had been promised, the right of asylum was inviolable. There was firm respect for the word of honour and for oral evidence, a feeling, almost, that once a thing was uttered it must happen. In true Semitic style, oral evidence was given greater credence than written evidence. In point of fact, there is precious little in the way of written documents in the life of a nomad; the people make up for it by their natural bent for eloquence and poetry; to this the beauty and suppleness of Arabic lend themselves admirably.

It is safe to say that the Arab people, prior to the seventh century, had acquired from their past, and from the kind of life they led, the beginnings of a real culture. Later on, the pre-Islamic era was to be nicknamed *jahiliyya*, which means ignorance. But this should not be taken so much to mean that they were barbarous people as that they did not know the One God and that they had not received a "revelation" from God. True enough, by comparison with the great Byzantine and Persian Empires with their magnificent religious, literary and scientific traditions, these beginnings of Arab culture are more like barely cleared land still waiting for the seed to be sown in it. One would have expected the seed to be brought straight in from beyond the frontiers and that, at some point in the triumphant advance of Byzantium or

[1] It may be considered as the forerunner of *mutuwwa*, "knightly honour", which Muslim tradition fostered; and *futuwa*, the "pact of honour" which held together all the members of a brotherhood, a body of artisans or an armed band.

Persia, Arabia would have come under their sway. But those imperial powers were already on the wane. And so it was to be from within, from Arab sources and in the Arabic tongue that a great power would arise, transforming these merchant nomads into the leaven of a great religious, cultural and juridico-political entity that would stretch eastwards to Indonesia and westwards to the Niger coast.

MOHAMMED AND THE RISE OF ISLAM

Mecca

Mohammed, of the Quraish tribe and the Banu Hashim clan, was born at Mecca in the year A.D. 570[2] The Banu Hashim clan was highly respected and allied to influential circles, but it would seem to have been greatly impoverished. It was not one of the ruling families. Mohammed never knew his father, for he died before he was born. He lost his mother when he was five or six years old. Three or four years later his grandfather, Abd al-Muttalib, died.

Mohammed the orphan grew up in poverty, entrusted to the care of several uncles, or more likely, to one of them whose name was also Abd al-Muttalib. He had a Beduin nurse, of whom Muslim tradition speaks with affection. With her he led the life of a nomad. In his youth and early manhood he lived at Mecca and was employed in connection with the trading caravans, which were the chief source of municipal funds. He was engaged by Khadija, the young widow of a rich merchant. It appears that he looked after her business for her. Then, although she was considerably older than he was, he married her. As long as she lived he took no other wife. They had four daughters and probably several sons who died quite young.

The sources emphasize the honesty and wisdom of

[2] Other dates have been put forward, 567, 569, 572, 573. For the social, economic and political background to the origins and expansion of Islam, see, W. Montgomery Watt, *Muhammad at Mecca* (Oxford, 1953), and *Muhammad at Medina* (Oxford, 1956).

Mohammed and his meditative disposition. He frequently retired for long spells to caves in Mount Hira, close to Mecca. It was there that one day his first "revelation" "descended" on him, at first frightening and disquietening him. According to the most frequently accepted Muslim tradition, this "revelation" was to become the ninety-sixth *Sura* of the Koran: "Recite in the name of thy Lord who created—who created man from clots of blood—Recite, for thy Lord is most beneficent—who hath taught the use of the pen—hath taught man that which he knoweth not."

Frightened and fearing he might be a prey to illusions, Mohammed confided in Khadija. She believed he was genuine and had faith in the words of the "revelation". Other "revelations" followed, and a small group of followers was formed: Ali ben Abu Talib, Mohammed's young cousin, Zayd, his adopted son, Abu Bakr, the "trustworthy", the "just", one of the most important business men in Mecca. Mohammed, the "announcer", preached amidst the irony and growing hostility of the Meccans. For the wealthy Meccans realized that this new creed spelt the ruin of the traditional framework of their city. What they did not foresee was that this very framework, although limited to local transactions, lent itself to expansion: they could not foresee that the expansion of Islam would bring to the families of Mecca the benefits of an Umayyad Arab Empire. The moment of conversion for the great merchants—in the event it was not entirely free from a motive of gain, for all its sincerity—had not yet come.

Other than these earliest adherents, there were only lowly folk to listen to the new preacher. That, perhaps, was all to the credit of his teaching. The hostility of the people in influential positions became so menacing that Mohammed had to advise his followers to emigrate to Abyssinia, a country where the people believed in one God and whose ruler welcomed refugees. The only outstanding convert at this stage was the influential Umar Ibn al-Kattab. It was about this time that both Khadija and Abu Talib (the father of Ali) died. The latter had never become a Muslim but he gave Mohammed every protection. Mohammed himself, a widower abandoned by his clan and his tribe, made a precarious bid for safety in the oasis of Taif. He was pursued and barely managed to regain Mecca unscathed.

Thus for well-nigh ten years, his few adherents and his numerous opponents in Mecca heard the recital of the first *Suras* (chapters) of the Koran, telling how God is merciful, almighty, creator, remunerator, supreme and just judge, inaccessible, benevolent, ready to grant pardon; stressing relentlessly that the hour of judgement was at hand; proclaiming, in the face of the Meccan polytheism, that there is only one single God; promising paradise to the believers and the torments of hell to the unbelievers; claiming as predecessors a long line of prophets, especially those of the Bible, from Adam to Christ; affirming a living and vital continuity of this new faith with the faith of Abraham, the friend of God.

It is towards the end of Mohammed's preaching at Mecca that, so tradition alleges, two great events took place which were to be a constant stimulus to Muslim piety. The first is what has come to be known as the nocturnal journey of Mohammed from Mecca to Jerusalem. The other was his "ascension" from Jerusalem to the throne of God. Some people admit that this journey and "ascension" were "in spirit", but it is more widely held that they were miraculous, bodily phenomena.[3]

Hostility became more and more marked and the believers found themselves in a precarious situation. At the annual Meccan fair, Mohammed once met twelve merchants from Yathrib—the rich oasis of the north—and two years later another seventy-two of them. With them he made a pact

[3] The "nocturnal journey" is generally commemorated on the 27th of the month of *rajab*, the "ascension" on the 17th or, preferably, on the 17th of the month of *ramadan* or at the end of *ramadan* during the night of destiny (*laylat al-qadr*), when the heavens are supposed to open and angels come and go between heaven and earth.

whereby they would protect him and his believers, if need be by force. Thus Mohammed and his first adherents, the Companions of the Prophet, carried to Yathrib, Mecca's rival, the "word of God".

The State of Medina

The believers left Mecca in successive groups. Mohammed, Abu Bakr and, undoubtedly, Ali, were the last to leave. Thus came about the famous flight, the *Hegira*, of the Prophet and Abu Bakr, pursued by the Meccans and escaping thanks to the shelter of a cave. They reached Quba, a suburb of Yathrib, on September 24th, 622. This date marks the year one of the Mohammedan era (abbreviated as A.H.).

And indeed, this Hegira of Mohammed and his Companions, leaving their tribe and family and their native town to go and live in Yathrib, is the beginning of the Muslim Community. The bond of blood on which rested the whole concept of tribal life, was to be replaced by a bond rooted in a freely accepted religious pact. At Yathrib, which came to be known as Madinat al-Nabi, the City of the Prophet (Medina), Mohammed devised a society based on the spiritual fraternity of Meccan companions and "auxiliaries" of Medina. During the first two years, which were the most difficult, each auxiliary had to take one of the companions into his home and treat him exactly as his brother.

However, not all the inhabitants of Medina by any means were auxiliaries and Mohammed met with opposition from several families, for instance the Aus Allah. He had to fight "hypocrites", the people who grudgingly accepted the established state of affairs but were ever ready to act the traitor. Most outstanding amongst them was Abd Allah ben Ubaiy. Besides, the possessors of the Book, that is, the Christians and Jews, were far from giving him the support he had hoped for. The Christians at Medina were few in number and they were not influential. Although Mohammed had rejected the teaching of the Christian mysteries, he took a sympathetic attitude towards the Christians themselves.[4] But the Jews and the rich Judaized tribes were in violent opposition to the new religion. To this there was a tragic outcome and the "hypocrites", allied though they were to the Jews, did nothing to defend them.

After the year 5 A.H., there were still a few Jews in Medina, but they were no longer a threat to the unity of the young Muslim Community and its expansion throughout the Arabian Peninsula.

Each expulsion or extermination of a Jewish tribe followed closely on an episode in the struggle of the Prophet and his followers against the Meccans. This struggle was Mohammed's major preoccupation and only ceased with the reconciliation and conversion of his compatriots. Muslim traditions record in detail its battles and skirmishes. Muslim historians made studies of its strategy, poets have lauded the valiant deeds of the believers and recently Taha Hussein wrote a film scenario from it.

The main events of the struggle can be set down thus:

In the year 2 A.H., victory of Badr over the greatly superior Meccan forces. The Muslims attributed victory to a miraculous intervention. After Badr, expulsion of the Qainuqui Jews.

In 3 A.H., defeat of Uhud by a force of 3,000 under the Meccan Abu Sufyan. Soon after this the defeat and expulsion of the Jews of Nadir.

5 A.H., the battle of the Ditch. A force of 10,000, consisting of Meccans and their partisans, set out to besiege Medina. On the advice of Salmon, a Persian Christian (a Nestorian, who it seems, always remained a Christian) Mohammed had a ditch dug across the approaches to Medina. The attackers

[4] Thus the celebrated passage of the Koran, 5, 82: "Of all men thou wilt certainly find the Jews, and those who join other gods with God, to be the most intense in hatred of those who believe; and thou shalt certainly find those to be nearest in affection to those who believe, who say, We are Christians. This, because some of them are priests and monks, and because they are free from pride."

were disconcerted and soon retired. Shortly after this the Qurayza Jews were exterminated for collaboration with the enemy.

6 A.H., a treaty negotiated at Hudaybiya. This was the first time Meccans consented to negotiate with Muslims.

7 A.H., occupation of the rich Jewish oasis of Khaybar. Tradition has it that about this time Mohammed sent envoys to the King of the Persians, the Emperor of Byzantium, the Negus of Abyssinia, the Governor of Alexandria and others, to persuade them to embrace Islam.[5]

8 A.H., a return to Mecca—the first—for a limited pilgrimage (*umra*) brought about a certain number of conversions. Shortly after this, Mohammed violated a treaty with Mecca and led an army against the city. The Meccans negotiated and nearly all of them accepted Islam. Mohammed was lenient towards his erstwhile fellow citizens, even making them liberal gifts, but he demanded the destruction of all the idols in the Kaaba. The victorious battle of Hunain against insurgent tribes also belongs to this time.

9 to 10 A.H., the "year of embassies"; the submission and conversion of many Arab tribes.

10 A.H., the small enclaves of Christians and Jews in the north of the Arab Peninsula accepted Muslim protection. It was in this year that took place the trial, or ordeal, by execration (*mubahala*), which led to the pact between Mohammed and the Nestorian Christians in Najran.[6] It may be said that by this date the Muslim Community extended over the whole of Arabia. Conversions, it is true, were often half-hearted, and the new religious concepts, persistently proclaimed by the *Suras* of the Koran, were hard put to it to supplant the ancient tribal mentality. The task that Mohammed had undertaken was nevertheless reaching completion:

[5] The texts of these messages are supposed to be extant. Most Islamic scholars in the West look on them as apocryphal. A Muslim erudite, Muhammad Hamidullah, has set out to prove their authenticity and has edited them; *La vie du Prophète* (Paris, 1959).

[6] Cf. Supplementary Note II, at the end of this chapter.

to give the Arabs, on behalf of One God, a 'reading' (*quran*: Koran) in "clear" language (Arabic) and bring all believers together in complete fraternity. Mohammed had just sent Abu Bakr (some say Ali) on the great pilgrimage to Mecca (the *hajj*) with orders to clear the city once and for all of idolaters.[7] All that remained was to put the final seal on the supra-tribal unity by coming in person, he the rejected and exiled, to bear witness to the One God in the purified temple of the Kaaba.

For this year 10 A.H. is the year of the "farewell pilgrimage", known also as the "pilgrimage of Islam". Thus, towards the end of the year, Mohammed himself went on pilgrimage, the *hajj*, and the ceremonies and actions he performed were to be the pattern for the future generations. Tradition has it that during this pilgrimage Mohammed, riding a white camel, received a "revelation" so weighty that the camel's knees gave way; and the Prophet pronounced a sermon of great beauty, the text of which, with some variants, has been handed down to this day.

Nothing in this sermon suggests that Mohammed had any presentiment of his impending death. Yet it was to be his farewell discourse. A few months later he fell ill, probably with Medina fever, and he died in the arms of his favourite wife, Aysha, on the 13th day of the month of Rabi in the year 10 A.H. (Monday, June 8th, A.D. 632).

The "House" of the Prophet

There are numerous traditions (*hadith*) which tell in detail the life of Mohammed at Mecca and Medina. "Envoy of God" (*rasul*) and by the same token, head of the *umma*, Community-State, of believers, his way of life kept much of the rustic life of the Arab Beduins and caravan merchants. The first mosque, at Medina, was simply a yard with an arcade round it.

[7] Idolaters, unlike Christians and Jews, had no place in the Muslim commonwealth.

The reader will expect some details of Mohammed's family life. The Koran permits and regulates polygamy: four legitimate wives are allowed, plus concubines, "provided debauchery is guarded against". Traditionalists are quick to speak of the "prophetic privilege" allowing Mohammed a greater number of wives.

As we have seen, as long as Khadija was alive, he had but one wife. It was principally to provide for the upbringing of his daughters of this first marriage that he later married Sauda bent Zamara, a Quraysh widow, and it was not until after the *hegira*, at the time therefore when he was organizing the State of Medina, that he began to practise polygamy. In any case, when he died in 632 he had four legitimate wives, the number authorized by the Koran: Aysha, daughter of the faithful Abu Bakr, to whom he was betrothed when he was nine, and who was his favourite and played a noteworthy part in Muslim politics and the elaboration of traditions; Umm Samama, widow of one of his cousins who had been killed in the battle of Uhud; Hafsa, daughter of Umar, and Zaynab, daughter of his maternal aunt, who had first married his adopted son Zayd b. Thabit. The tale of the repudiation of Zaynab by Zayd at Mohammed's request is a celebrated page in Islamic history.[8] The five other women of his harem were given, for a variety of reasons, the rank of "honorary wives".

Special mention must be made of a Christian concubine of whom he was specially fond. She was Marya the Copt. She was the only one who gave him a son, the young Ibrahim. To Mohammed's great grief, the child died at the age of about six months. So the Prophet had no male descendant, a fact which pious Muslims interpret as a divine intervention to give Islam roots elsewhere than in the traditional Arab notions and sentiments. The Traditions speak with affection of his daughters, especially those born of his

[8] It owes its fame to the mention made of it in the Koran, 33, 37. Contrary to the ancient Arab custom, Muslim law allowed a man to marry the repudiated wife of his adopted son.

wife Khadija at Mecca, namely Ruqayya, Umm Kulthum, Zaynab, Fatima. The last of these, greatly beloved by her father, met with enmity from Aysha. She married Ali b. Abu Talib, who had no other wife while she lived, and was the mother of Hasan and Husayn. Fatima, Ali and their two sons, "people of the House of the Prophet" (*ahl al-bayt*), are venerated in Islam down to the present day and the heterodox Shiites pay them a special cult. Fatima felt the loss of her father cruelly. She did not long outlive him, dying in 633. To Shiite piety she is the mysterious prototype of the woman to be revered and invoked. It can be said that the Sunnite traditions brought about a belated conciliation between Fatima and Aysha in the hearts of the believers, for they hold them both together in special veneration.[9]

At Medina each of the Prophet's wives had her own miniature house, built in brick or clay and palm branches. The plainness of these buildings—and they were purposely so—became proverbial. Mohammed lived in these houses turn and turn about, and all he had when he wanted to be alone was a similar construction built above one of them or on the roof of the mosque. A passage in the Koran says that the spouses of the Prophet are "the mothers of the believers": once they became widows or were repudiated, they could not marry again and their behaviour was such as to be a model for all Muslim women.

The birth of the Community

By the time Mohammed died, it can be said that the entire Arabian Peninsula had become united in the Muslim faith. Mecca was once more the religious capital and towards that holy city all believers must turn at prayer.[10]

[9] Louis Massignon, *La Mubahala de Médine et l'hyperdulie de Fatima* (Paris, 1955).

[10] At the time of the *hegira*, the *gibla* (direction of prayer) was Jerusalem. A *hadith* says: "Jerusalem was the first *gibla* and will be the last," that is, at the end of time, after the apparition of the *Mahdi*—the announcer of the Judgement—and before the resurrection.

The Muslims at Medina besides being a Community were also a State. It is true that the texts of the Koran uttered by the Prophet at Medina continue as at Mecca to speak of God, One and Creator and Remunerator, and of the interior sentiments demanded in regard to God—reverential fear and confident self-surrender (which is the meaning of the Arabic word "Islam"). But at the same time they determine the life of the Community. Some Western writers have pointed out that the parts of the Koran produced at Mecca are in contradiction with those uttered at Medina, for the first, with great sincerity, contain a purely eschatological teaching, whereas the latter are preoccupied with organizing life in this world which represents a considerable compromise. But no Muslim would ever agree with such a suggestion. For the fervent Muslim there is perfect continuity between the Mecca and Medina *Suras*: the *hegira*, the exile and flight of Mohammed and his Companions, links up at one and the same time with the imminence of the last hour and "the rights of God and man"[11] which have to be promoted in this world.

No provision had been made for Mohammed's successor, so that when he died the supra-tribal bond, with which he had knit together all believers, was in danger of dissolution. There was so much dissension among the Muslims that a whole day went by before the Prophet's body could be buried. It was buried in the ground underneath the dwelling of Aysha, the place where he died. Very soon Abu Bakr, the father of Aysha, one of the earliest Companions, succeeded in taking the situation in hand and renewed the pact between the Meccans and the Medinans. The history of the vast expansion of the Muslim Community was about to unfold.

[11] *Huquq Allah wa huquq admiyyin.* This is an expression which we shall often refer to in the study of the Muslim Community and commonwealth.

THE KORAN

The final seal of prophecy

From its very inception Islam was to be directly centred on the Koran. For the Christian, Christ came to perfect all things, and revelation is brought to a close with the death of the last of the apostles. For the Muslim, it is the Koran that completes and closes the earthly cycle of the Envoys of God. The Koran was spoken by the Prophet, it was stored safely in the memory of the Companions, written down by such as were able to write and eventually it was all drawn up in an official recension by Uthman, the third of the caliphs.

The 114 chapters (*Suras*) of the Koran were arranged according to their length, the shortest first, and the whole text was prefaced by the *Sura* called *al-Fatiha*, the "opening", which became the model of Islamic prayer:

> Praise be to God, Lord of the worlds!
> The compassionate, the merciful!
> King on the day of reckoning!
> Thee only do we worship, and to thee do we cry for help.
> Guide thou us on the straight path,
> The path of those to whom thou hast been gracious;
> With whom thou are not angry, and who go not astray.

There is only one version of the Koran as far as the consonants of the text are concerned, though there are variations in the vowel-points here and there and, consequently, slightly different "readings".

The liturgical recitation and singing of the Koran to the tones of the *tajwid* are both a science and an art, practised by the bearers of the Koran, pious men who are able to recite and sing every line of the book by heart.

Each of the chapters of the Koran, every one of its 6,226 verses, are looked on as "signs from God" (*ayat Allah*) and the sincere Muslim regards it as a supernatural dictation communicated to Mohammed, the inspired Prophet. It is, for the Muslim, the subsistent word of God, the distinction between good and evil. To the lips and the heart of the believer, it is as "sweet as honey". The Prophet, the whole Community after him, is consecrated to the service of this word. Mohammed himself is first and foremost the messenger, the "warner", to whom the transmission of this deposit is entrusted. As Louis Massignon puts it, the Muslims have always considered that the excellence of the literary form of the Koran is the ultimate proof of the personal prophetic inspiration of Mohammed: for them the style is a miracle surpassing all physical miracles. And so the unsurpassable beauty of the Koran, in the eyes of Islam, is its own witness to its authenticity.

The Koran recognizes that the Torah and the Gospel are "revealed". It accuses the Jews and Christians of falsifying their books, but despite this they remain "keepers of the Scriptures". The later teaching of Islam declared that the word of God is Torah and Gospel and Koran. But Mohammed is the "seal of the Prophets",[12] so much so that the Koran sums up all anterior prophecies and gives them a definitive form.

But in the course of all this, the Koran does not, as one might expect, retrace God's plan for mankind. The story of mankind is not presented as a progressive unfolding of events but as a succession of disjointed interventions on the part of God. These, through the voice of the prophets, reiterate the truths and the conditions set down in the primordial covenant, leading on to the fulfilment of that covenant at the supreme hour.

The primordial covenant is the pact which God, from eternity, before the creation of bodies, granted to Adam's race. "Am I not, said he, your Lord? They said, Yes, we witness it. This we did, lest ye should say on the day of Resurrection, Truly, of this were we heedless, because uninformed."[13]

[12] Koran, 33, 40.
[13] Koran, 7, 172.

This self-same covenant, a witness rendered to God, was recalled by each of the prophets against the incredulity and wickedness of men. It reaches its culminating point in the faith of Abraham and is of the very essence of the Muslim Community.

Thus the entire Koran looks towards man's ultimate end and is dominated by eschatology. Its teaching can be grouped under two heads, each of which can be subdivided into two parts. Under the first head comes what may be termed a non-temporal or supra-temporal teaching. This deals, on the one hand, with the inaccessible mystery of God-One and, on the other, with the imminence of the hour of annihilation, the resurrection, the great "gathering", the final judgement, the torments promised to the reproved and the reward promised to the elect. Under the second head come the disjointed temporal events identified with the successive prophetic missions; and lastly there is the delineation of the pattern of life within the framework of Muslim prophecy.

God

The Koran is not a theological exposition of the existence of God, his nature and attributes. God is there the unfathomed mystery, the inaccessible, ascertained in his transcendent perfections and in his interventions in the world. Three themes are prevalent throughout; they have to be taken as part of one whole. 1. God is the creator, judge and remunerator; 2. He is unique (*wahid*) and one in himself (*ahad*); 3. He is at one and the same time omnipotent and merciful. He is Lord of the worlds, the Lord of the East and the West, in his omnipotence which is accepted unquestioningly. This, in its turn, draws the believer to see in him a protector and to laud this divine power of mercy and forgiveness: a thought most vividly emphasized in the Koran.

The absolute precept of love, Thou shalt love the Lord thy God with thy whole soul, is not formulated in the Koran. What is brought out is, first of all, the inscrutable sovereignty of God and then, total and blind surrender. A text of the Medina period identifies this surrender to God (*Islam*) with religion (*din*) itself. But from the first Meccan period, the believer is exhorted to trust to the favours of the Lord.[14]

The prophetic revelation commands man to reflect on the signs of the universe and discover in them the signs of God.[15] Marvellous are the order and harmony, without blemish, of the world. Man is exposed to the temptation of adoring them, but he must come to recognize, as the prophet Abraham did, that there is nothing created that does not perish (Koran 6, 75). Guided by God, man's reason will discover in the perishable world the irrefutable evidence of the necessary and transcendent existence of the Creator.

It is the perfections showing forth his unicity and omnipotence in regard to this order in the world that God reveals. He possesses the most beauteous names. He is One and Unique, the Living One, the Subsistent, the True-Reality, the Sublime, the Most High, the Redoubtable, the Light and Light upon light, the absolute Creator who ceases not to create, the one unlike all created things, he that Heareth, the All-seeing, the Omniscient, the Witness, the Benefactor, the Protector, the Generous, the Merciful, the Pardoner who ceases not to absolve, the Compassionate, the Well-wisher, the best of Judges. . . . Muslim piety has carefully picked out from the text of the Koran the "most Beauteous Names" and, with others from tradition, brought the list to ninety-nine: these are still committed to memory and made the subject of meditation.

Last ends and final reckoning

The hour of reckoning is ever imminent and, when it strikes, man, in response to the primordial pact, will find himself face to face with his Lord. In verses written like psalms,

[14] Koran, 5, 3 and 93, 11.
[15] Koran, 2, 118 and many other passages.

with almost painful and breathless insistency, the Meccan *Suras* tell of the terrors of the judgement and the severance of the wicked from the just, with hell and the pleasures of heaven allotted accordingly. The decree of God is efficacious and supreme, and man must know that each of his actions carries its tale of reward for good and punishment for evil (Koran, 2, 286).

In this treatment of the last day, the Koran keeps two things constantly in perspective: the implacable omnipotence of God "who has no account to give of himself" and the just retribution of the works of man.

Such passages have been suspected as "contradictory verses" and have given rise to controversy among the Muslim schools themselves. In point of fact, they are contrasting and complementary statements, by which the Koran endeavours to instil into the heart of the believer the behaviour exacted by his relationship to God. For the Koran does not set itself the theological problem of predestination nor the philosophical problem of the nature of the freedom of human acts. Indeed, it does not set itself problems at all. What it is doing is emphasizing the mystery of the relationship between the creature and the Creator. Even the problem of the nature of evil is not taken up. "It is God who hath created thee and all that thou hath done" (Koran, 52, 96). And yet "Whatever good betideth thee is from God, and whatever evil betideth thee is from thyself" (Koran, 4, 79).

The following distinction is noteworthy. There is the fulfilment of divine decrees, in the temporal sphere, in this world, and in that man is awarded according to his works and merits: reward promised to the just, chastisement to those who "turn their back" (Koran, 92, 16). The reprobate are those who refuse divine help. On the day of judgement every soul shall be judged according to its deserts (Koran, 40, 17).

But then there are also the immutable decrees of God in the non-temporal sphere, and in that no "conditions" can be posited to the divine will and commandments. God grants his favours to whom he will. And there is the telling assertion: "He leads astray whom he will and guides whom he will." And the man whom God leads astray can have neither patron nor guide. Twice we encounter a figurative expression characteristically Semitic and reminiscent of Isaias (6. 9–10): "Truly we have thrown veils over their hearts lest they should understand and into their ears a heaviness" (Koran, 18, 57) and, "He whom God causes wilfully to err, and whose ears and whose heart he hath sealed up, and over whose sight he hath placed a veil" (Koran, 45, 23). The context of these two verses emphasizes the wickedness of those who turn away from the signs of the Lord. "They have no patron but themselves", says *Sura* 19, 45.

The responsibility of man and the absolute decree of God, these are two capital assertions running through the teaching, each reaching, still with no attempt at conciliation, their culminating point in the announcement of the judgement, where before the eyes of all shall shine forth the omnipotence and the mystery of the Most High God, who knows each and every creature and the thoughts of man.

The prophets

The second teaching of the Koran, still keeping in sight the imminent hour, is found, as it were, at the meeting point of the eschatological world and the succession of temporal events. First of these are the history of the prophets of the Old and New Testaments and reference to certain of the prophets among non-Biblical peoples.

As early as the first Meccan *Suras* the great biblical personages and the peoples of *Thamud* are recalled. The second and third Meccan periods interweave the announcement of the judgement and the decrees of God towards the nations, the *Thamud* and the *Ad*; they give particular emphasis to the mission of Noah, Abraham, Moses and Jesus. The Medina

Suras describe the story of Adam and dwell at great length on the above-mentioned prophets.

But throughout these similarities and divergences and passages parallel to those of the Haggadah or to apocryphal gospels, a critical examination of "sources" is not even envisaged by the Muslim commentators. For, to their way of thinking, all revelation is given word for word to the prophet upon whom it "descends". Hence, if there is identity between the Koran and the texts of the "possessors" of the Scriptures, it is because, according to Muslims, God has repeated to the Prophet of Islam, through the agency of the angel of revelation,[16] what he had already communicated to previous prophets. If there are divergences, it is either because the manner of the teaching is different or because the ancient Laws have since been distorted by man. In any case it is the text of the Koran, seal of all prophecy, that must be taken as authentic.

Of all the prophets brought into the Koran, predominance is given to those called the "apostles endowed with constancy". These are, in chronological order, Noah, whose ark symbolizes the maintenance and renewal of the primordial pact; Abraham, the friend of God, Moses, the interlocutor of God; Jesus, son of Mary and "Word of God". Each of them became the prototype of a religious disposition. Abraham is the witness to faith in the Unique and is the breaker of idols. With Ismael he rebuilt and purified the temple of the Kaaba, which had been destroyed by the deluge. He was ready to sacrifice that very Son whom God had given him in answer to his prayer. The "solemn sacrifice" which

[16] "The faithful spirit" (26, 192); "the spirit of sanctity" (16, 102). In 2, 97 it is the Angel Gabriel who is mentioned. The ministry of the angel, sometimes seen by Mohammed, sometimes only heard by him, was to become for Islam the specific modality of prophetic revelation. It is this that distinguishes it from personal divine inspiration, which may also be experienced by a prophet but also by some just or holy man who is not a prophet. "Inspiration" pure and simple does not imply a mission to transmit a religious law to men.

was offered instead is perpetuated in the Community by divine command. It is thus that the central Muslim religious act, the sacrificial pilgrimage at Mecca, was to be linked with the memory of Abraham. Moses retired to the desert for forty days. God spoke to him in the burning bush on the mountain and gave him the Torah for the children of Israel. And when, yearning for God, Moses asked to see him face to face, the Lord replied: "Thou shalt not see me; but look towards the mountain and, if it abide firm in its place, then shalt thou see me." And when God manifested himself to the mountain he turned it to dust! And Moses fell in a swoon (7, 139). Among the passages referring to Jesus in the Koran, two stand out from the rest: his birth beneath a palm tree and the laden table that came down from heaven at his prayer when the apostles asked him for a sign.

It is to this faith of Abraham that the faith-and-witness in the Unique, demanded of the believer, looks back as to its type and exemplar. Islam has unremittingly claimed Abraham as its father, according to the flesh through Hagar and Ismael, spiritually through the recovery of faith. In the face of all the revolts and apostasies of the peoples visited by the prophets, the Koran proclaims a fundamental identity between the Announcement that sums up all Announcements and the faith of Abraham. The text does not give the name of the son whom Abraham was asked to sacrifice. Some traditions name Isaac, but the common teaching speaks only of the sacrifice of Ismael.

Code of conduct

This last Annunciation, the Koran, is thus given for the last of the "disjointed" temporal events, the one that comes before the great day of reckoning. Thus, for this last "fission of time", it hands the world to the believer and organizes the Community, whose task it is to bear witness. The Medina *Suras*, regulating social and civic relationships, do not suggest to the Muslim a lapse into the temporal and a surrender to man's reason. Enshrined in the uniformity of the Islamic faith, they are still a manifestation of the divine will.

Such is the final aspect of the teaching of the Koran. It includes the "pillars" of cult, for the individual and for society, demanded of the Community as such. There, too, we find in a considerably abbreviated form the basis of the administrative framework of the commonwealth: he who is in command is the instrument of God and his orders must be obeyed: he in turn must consult his subordinates and the believers must consult each other. The text makes all manner of applications and elucidations possible. We find also, in this part of the teaching, the regulations about marriage, wills, food, all of which have decisive bearing on "living together". Lastly, there are here the regulations regarding the "combat in the way of God" by which the "rights of God and man" are to be established throughout the world.

This rather piecemeal account does not claim to be a summary of the Koran. For the pious Muslim the Koran knows of no summary, for it is an entity, "a solid mass", like God himself. It is quite certain that no translation can convey the vibrant religious sentiment experienced by a Muslim on reading the text of the Koran. It is written in prose and is indeed the earliest extant Arabic prose text. A rhythmic prose, if you will, but one whose pulse seems to beat to a constant awareness of a transcendent being. The semantic genius of the Arabic sentence lends flashes of colour and life to the stark theocentricity of the Koran.

APPENDIX TO CHAPTER I

THE KORAN AND CHRISTIAN DOGMAS

We have spoken of the extreme severity with which the Koran treated the Jews of Medina who were accused of collaborating with Mohammed's enemies in Mecca and we have noted the sympathetic attitude he took towards those who say: "We are Christians" (Koran, 5, 82). Judging from this verse, it would seem that Christians were clearly distinguished from "associators" (*mushrikun*), who "give associates to God". This expression in the Koran means putting other beings on a footing with God, thus denying that he is the only One God. There are many verses, however, belonging to the Medina period in particular, which exhort Christians not to fall into this crime of "associating" but to bear witness to the one and only God.

Indeed, at various times, passages from the Koran have been looked on by Muslim apologists as the refutation of the Christian dogma of the Trinity and Incarnation. But when we come to examine these passages more closely, we discover that their statement of the Christian dogmas they propose to refute is far from accurate. What they are refuting is not orthodox Christian belief at all but heretical views which the Church herself repudiates.

Thus, in regard to the Trinity: "Say not Three: God is one only divinity" (Koran, 4, 169). And in another *Sura* (5, 177) we read: "They surely are infidels who say God is the third of three." The way the Incarnation is represented varies. Sometimes Christ is spoken of as a human person clad in divinity —a statement suggestive of the Nestorian heresy. Sometimes, and this is more frequent, he is spoken of as a humano-divine person engendered according to the flesh by the divinity itself. Thus, 4, 177: "Far be it from him that he should have a son." And 5, 16: "O Jesus, son of Mary, hast thou said unto mankind, Take me and my mother as two Gods beside God?"

We can understand how these misstatements of Christian dogma come to be made, if we remember that the Koran was inveighing against the pantheon in the Kaaba at Mecca, where the "sons and daughters of God" were idolatrously worshipped. Hence the very expression "son of God" was taboo. It is quite certain that later Muslim apologists read into these texts a refutation of Christian dogmas. But it is equally certain that not one of the Koranic texts in question gives an accurate account of Christian teaching. Hence it would be more correct to say that the Koran does not deal with Christian teaching at all, rather than to say that it repudiates it.

We find the same situation occurring at a later period. Muslims who later sought to refute Christian dogma wrongly took the definition of the Trinity to mean that there was plurality of substances in God. On the other hand, Muslim writers who set out to take a sympathetic approach to Christianity by showing that Christians were indeed monotheists—thus, Ghazali, Ibn Rushd, Ibn Qayyim—did little else than present the Trinity as erroneously taught by the Modalists and spoke of the Incarnation as merely the language of theopathy.

The Muslim distrust of Christianity is not the direct result of the study and refutation of Christian teaching; it merely springs from an obsessing urge to defend the transcendence of divine unity. Now, God in the Koran is indeed *the* God (Allah), one in his deity and in nature—a total mystery in his immanent life. It is because they are looked on as an affront to the divine *nature* that Christian dogmas are brushed aside. This is so true that, although the unity of *substance*, neither begetting nor begot, is formulated in both Christian and Islamic belief, Muslims are all too ready to think that Christians do not accept it or at least distort it.

Muslim piety towards Christ and his mother, based on the Koran, is remarkable. There is a store of narratives, reminiscent of the apocryphal Gospels: the story of Mary in the Temple, her marriage to Joseph (these passages belong to the Medinan epoch), the birth of Christ under a desert palm-tree and the witness he bears to his mother from the moment he came into the world (second Meccan epoch), the miracles supposed to have been performed by our Lord as a child and a youth (Medina).

But in the Medinan *Suras* there is a solemn affirmation of the virgin birth of Christ and the assertion that Christ *is* the "Word of God" (*Kalimat Allah*), conveyed by God to Mary, and a "spirit proceeding from God" (Koran, 4, 177). He is "strengthened by the spirit of sanctity" and "his name is the messiah" (3, 45). Yet all this is without any allusion to the Incarnation. In the line of the prophets, Christ is the only one who is "after the image of Adam" (3, 59). He is thus presented in unparalleled grandeur. So true is this, that the Sufis (Ibn Arabi) took Christ as portrayed in the Koran as a rule of life, and the Tirmidhi considered him to be the "seal of sanctity". The creative word of God *kun* ("let there be") was uttered in the Koran for the creation of the world, the creation of Adam and the conception of Christ.

But the function of the "son of Mary" is that of every prophet: to transmit the warning of God. The Koran mentions the disciples (apostles) of Christ. It lays stress on his preaching. In the Koran he is "different from other men", for he is born of the Word of God conveyed to Mary; but he is prophet among the prophets, one of the greatest of them, and his task is not yet ended, since he is to return at the end of time.

For Christ has been "lifted up to God". The cross, as Christians teach it, remains a scandal in Islam. There is the celebrated text of *Sura* 3, 157: "They neither killed nor crucified him; it had only the appearance of it." A little further on in the same *Sura*, the text speaks mysteriously of the death of Christ, and commentators have understood this to mean a death which Jesus will undergo at the end of time. A Shiite tradition adds to the words "they neither killed, etc." the following gloss: "They did not kill his soul, his person." But the general interpretation throughout Islam has always been of a Docetist variety: "substitution" of Christ on the cross, followed by an assumption—not, be it noted, a resurrection.

Lastly, while Islam records the Fall of Adam in the

Garden (second *Sura*), the dogma of original sin is wanting. Hence, there could be no place in Islamic teaching for the dogma of redemption. Indeed whereas the Koran takes up and condemns points regarding such Christian dogmas as the Trinity and the Incarnation (in a mistaken and heretical form, as we have seen), it does not so much as mention the dogma of redemption.

MOHAMMED AND THE CHRISTIANS OF NAJRAN

Muslim traditions have preserved a vivid account of the meeting of Mohammed and the Nestorian Christians of Najran and the subsequent pact, the first to be concluded between the infant Muslim Community and a Christian community. It is worth relating in some detail.

Najran is a region and a city in the north of the Yemen, that is, in the southern region of the Arabian Peninsula. Economically it was a region of very great importance, for it was crossed by the caravan routes running from Hadramaut to the eastern shores of the Mediterranean. When Islam first came into being, Najran was a sort of small Christian (Nestorian) republic.

A Muslim tradition (*hadith*) recorded in several extant texts of the second century A.H. tells of an event, to all appearances historically vouched for, which happened in the year 10 A.H., that is, at the end of the year known as the year of Embassies.

When the Muslim state spread down to the Yemen, the people of Najran sent an embassy to Medina—seventy horsemen, fourteen nobles among them, led by the chief of the artisans, the supervisor of the caravans and the bishop, all clad in their gala finery of brocade. They came in among the people of the city and Mohammed allowed them to go into the mosque and pray, turning towards the east. Then they were received in audience. Mohammed upbraided them for believing in the divinity of Christ and tried to convert them to Islam. The discussion became heated, and Mohammed, in line with the Koran, 3, 54, proposed settling the matter next morning by "ordeal by execration". At the meeting, the leaders of the Najran Christians declared that they would not have recourse to this method. Terms were discussed and a pact signed by which they placed themselves under the protection of Mohammed.

The two essential facts here are the recourse to ordeal and the terms of the pact. Ordeal by execration, mutual malediction, is called in Arabic *mubahala*, "judgement of God". It has a foundation in the Koran, for *Sura* 3, 54 says: "As for those who dispute with thee about him (Christ), after thou hast acquired sure knowledge, summon our sons and your sons, and our wives and your wives, ourselves and yourselves, and then let us call down mutual imprecations, invoking the malediction of God upon those that lie." This is all performed according to a set mime and ritual.

Now, this passage is immediately preceded by a statement about Christ, that, like Adam, he was created from clay. May we then suppose that the text we have quoted from the Koran (3, 54) is an abbreviated account of the actual proposal of "ordeal" made to the Najranites by Mohammed? In the context of the Koran, as in the discussion with the Najranites, it is a question of the divinity of Christ. But two things must be noted here: first, the expression "like Adam, he was created from clay" bears directly on the human *nature* of Christ, and second, the Najranites were Nestorians and, therefore, held that there were in Christ two distinct *persons*, one human and one divine. Thus the point at issue on this famous occasion at Najran could not have been the pivotal Christian mystery of the one divine person in Christ. No wonder the Najranites evaded the challenge.

As we read the account of this scene, our minds travel across the centuries to St Francis of Assisi, at the court of the Sultan, insisting on recourse to *mubahala*. It was the Muslim sovereign on this occasion who evaded the challenge!

But away back in the year 10 A.H., Mohammed had prepared the *mubahala* with great solemnity. He came to the meeting, as the Koran stipulates, surrounded by his own folk. These, according to tradition, were his grandsons Hasan and Husayn, his daughter Fatima, his son-in-law Ali. The story of this *mubahala* was specially cherished by the Shiites: there, in this solemn affirmation of the unity of the divine nature, stood together the "five" and the "people of the House". Miniatures portray Mohammed facing the Najranites, folding in his cloak his four co-witnesses and guarantors, with lightning flashing from his forehead.

The pact between Mohammed and the Najranites was binding even after the death of Mohammed. The Najranites kept faith with the Alid guarantors whom Mohammed had gathered around him. In the year 11 A.H., southern Arabia was momentarily shaken by rebellions but the Najranites took no part in them. In the year 40 A.H. they refused to associate themselves with the malediction against Ali pronounced by Muaqiya, founder of the Umayyad dynasty.

The courtesy shown to the Najranites in the text of the pact is significant. In return for reasonable demands in the matter of taxation and services, "the protection of God and the guarantee of the Prophet Mohammed, Envoy of God, go out to Najran and its surrounds, on their possessions, their persons, their worship, those at home and those abroad, their sanctuaries and all things great and small that are theirs. No bishop shall be deposed from his see, no monk driven from his monastery, no priest from his parish. No humiliation shall weigh on them nor any vengeance incurred before this submission. They shall not be summoned nor subject to tithe. No army shall tread their land. And when any one of them shall claim his rights, justice shall hold sway amongst them. They shall not oppress nor be oppressed.

And any who henceforth practise usury will forfeit my protection. No man amongst them shall be held responsible for the fault of another. . . ."

That, of course, was a pact mutually and freely entered upon: it did not come after battle and defeat. When the "people of the Book" (Jews or Christians) submitted after armed conflict, they might meet with more severe treatment, as the Koran provides. Be that as it may, we can readily understand why present-day Muslim reformers look to the Najran pact, enhanced as it is by its author, Mohammed himself, as a possible basis for promoting a whole-hearted respect for minority groups, in a spirit of civic and social equality, within the Muslim commonwealth.

CHAPTER II

HISTORICAL DEVELOPMENT: THE RISE AND FALL OF MUSLIM POWER

In the year 622 came the *hegira*, the flight of a handful of fugitives from Mecca. In 632, the conversion of Mecca to Islam was only just accomplished and Mohammed died. By 732 the Muslim Empire stretched from the lower reaches and delta of the Indus right across to Gaul where, on a Saturday in October, a rampart of Frankish infantry and cavalry under Charles Martel stood between Tours and Poitiers before which the onrush of the tide of Islam was halted.

From its very first years, Islam presents the aspect of a religion with its dogmas and its precepts, a terrestrial city expanding to a worldwide empire and a way of life imposing its own social and cultural attitude. It would be impossible here to follow in all its complex detail this threefold development. We shall insist on Islam as a religious phenomenon and as a cultural and social entity. But before we do that, we must give a rapid sketch of its history, so as to have a clear perspective of our subject.

When Mohammed died, it was his son-in-law, Abu Bakr, the "just", the "veracious", who brought unity to Mecca and

Medina once more, and in this he was helped by Umar Ibn al-Khattab. The original pact, then, between the faithful of these two holy cities was thus revived. Abu Bakr was proclaimed the Prophet's representative, Khalifat al-Nabi, the caliph, and the important members of the Community acknowledged his authority and gave him their allegiance. Thus the caliphate was launched.

Abu Bakr ruled for two years (632–4). On his deathbed he appointed as his successor Umar Ibn al-Khattab, who was also accepted by the notables of the Community. He was to remain throughout history the prototype of all caliphs. In 644 he was stabbed by a Persian Christian. Six electors were designated to decide on his successor. They chose Uthman, a feeble old man, who was one of Mohammed's sons-in-law. It was Uthman who compiled the definitive *corpus* of the scattered Koranic texts. Political intrigues soon arose. Uthman was taxed with nepotism and with relaxing the pure Muslim observance. He was assassinated in 656, by Muslims. In face of the opposition of Aysha, these gave the throne to Ali Ibn Abi Talib, cousin of Mohammed and husband of his daughter Fatima. The close partisans of Ali declared him to be the only legitimate caliph, because he was a member of the "family of the Prophet". In 655, however, he was obliged to abdicate and, in 661, he died from a wound inflicted with a poisoned sword.

The years 632–65, which we have just sketched, were to be of capital importance in the history of Islam. The State of Medina, which had grown from no other soil than the Koran, had about it the aura of its hallowed origins. This the first four caliphs kept alive. The caliphate was not dynastic. Although there was no clearly defined procedure, each caliph was chosen by the notables, "those who bind and loose", the representatives of the Community. Their standards and customs, their notion of the commandments, remained those of the Arab tribes, except that now they were unified and inspired by a new faith. "Revelation" reached completion with the death of the Prophet and each successive caliph was the servant of the Koran. His function was to apply the Koranic law alike in political and social life and in religious practice. He was the Imam, who normally presides at prayer and "walks at the head of the people"; he stands in the Prophet's stead and, using the title first adopted by Umar I, is the chief, the "commander of the believers". Muslim piety and traditions (Sunnite) were to hold the first four caliphs in hallowed memory; they alone are the "enlightened" (*rashidun*) caliphs, they alone made the Muslim Community all that it should be.

We may note two essential features which were to have an inescapable bearing on the future. First, territorial expansion. Several Arab tribes had been superficially Islamized in the Prophet's lifetime and seceded as soon as he died. During the two years following his reign, Abu Bakr succeeded in establishing a large measure of unity in the Arabian peninsula. But that did not mean the end of tribal feuds. Umar I played on the ambitions and covetousness of the tribes, by entrusting them with the conquest of foreign territories that resisted Islam. It was thus that the great Arab Muslim cavalcades began. They owed much to the religious enthusiasm, the military courage and the urge for power and wealth of the Arabs, and to the cunning and rivalry of their war chiefs. Much to their purpose also was the weakness of the Byzantine and Persian Empires, with their internal religious and racial conflicts. Damascus and Alexandria were besieged, but held out. It was the Christians who opened the gates of these cities to the Muslims—Damascus in 636 and Alexandria in 642. To the east, Chaldea and Assyria succumbed to the Arab troops at the battle of Qadissiyya, 637; the Iranian Empire fell to them at Nihawend (641–2) and by 643 they stood at the frontiers of India.

The second event was to leave its mark on Islam for centuries to come. When Syria was conquered, Umar entrusted its government to Muawiya. He was a Meccan who had come late to Islam. His father was the wealthy Abu Sufyan, long the sworn enemy of Mohammed. Muawiya carried the ambition of the great caravan merchants of Mecca to the limits of the whole of the known world. He was the cousin of Uthman, the caliph who had been assassinated, and he refused to acknowledge Ali. Ali had first of all to conquer Iraq and this he did with the support of Egypt. But Syria, under Muawiya, persisted in standing aloof. The decisive encounter occurred at Siffin, in 655 (the year 37 A.H.). Ali had almost won the day, when suddenly Muawiya, hooking pages of the Koran to the soldiers' lances, appealed to the "judgement of God". Ali had no choice but to come to terms. The outcome for Ali was tragic. Even his most ardent partisans left him and went off to the borders of Mesopotamia and Iran. They are the first dissidents or schismatics we come across and are known as *Khawarij* (Kharijites), the "leavers", the "separated". The groups who remained faithful to Ali are the "partisans", the Shiites.

The *Shiat Ali*, the Ali Party, is the second schism. After the show of arbitration which brought to a close the clash at Siffin, Muawiya succeeded in getting Ali deposed and had himself proclaimed caliph by the Syrians. Although Ali struggled successfully against the Kharijites, the Muslims as a whole, Iraq and then Egypt, eventually recognized Muawiya as the one lawful caliph. In vain did Ali withstand the partisans of Muawiya and it was a Kharijite who assassinated him in 661.

There were thus two extremes: on the one hand, unbending Kharijites, who were ready to accept as caliph any Muslim of merit, and on the other hand, the Shiites, who made so much of their attachment to Ali and his descendants that in course of time a religious devotion grew up towards him. Indeed, the extremists deified him. But between the two extremes stood the mass of the Muslims. They had accepted Muawiya as caliph and they became firm adherents of the orthodox Sunna, that is to say, "the practice of the

Prophet", *sunnat al-Nabi*. But Muawiya did something further: he replaced the elected caliphate with what amounted to dynastic succession. The "reformers", who were ever the animators of Sunna, reproached Muawiya with putting a temporal royalty in the place of the caliphate. Rashid Rida, one of the strictest of contemporary reformers (he died in 1935), went so far as to say that, ever since the battle of Siffin, the Muslim caliphate has been radically illegitimate.

UMAYYAD EMPIRE (661–750)

Whether called caliphate or temporal royalty, the dynasty that came into being in 37 A.H. is known to history as the Umayyad Dynasty, from the Banu Umayya, the Meccan family to which Muawiya belonged. Its capital was transferred from Medina to Damascus, where the caliphs were, to their advantage, in contact with the administrative and cultural traditions of the Byzantine Empire.

Muawiya saw to it that his son Yazid was designated as his successor to the throne. But Yazid's succession was not ensured as easily as all that. There were two other claimants. The first of them was soon overcome, but the circumstances of his death were such as to leave their mark on Muslim beliefs. It happened this way. Hasan, the eldest son of Ali and Fatima, died young at Medina. His youngest brother, Husayn, fled from Medina with a feeble escort, to join his supporters at Kufa. But the troops of Yazid soon caught up with him and surrounded him and he was hacked down on the battlefield. Fatima, as we have seen, died shortly after her father, probably in 633. With the slaughter of Husayn there went the last of the "people of the House" (*ahl al-bayt*), Ali, Fatima, Hasan and Husayn, the four whom, according to the cherished Shiite tradition, Mohammed had covered with his mantle at the Mubahala. In the eyes of their adepts, the assassination of Ali and the slaughter of Husayn were both the death of martyrdom "in the way to God". The "passion of Husayn" was for centuries to inspire Shiite prayer and piety and Kerbela (Iraq) and Meshed (Iran), where the "tombs of the martyrs" are, became in the highest degree "holy cities" of Shia.

The other rival to the Umayyads was to leave scarcely any trace in Islamic religious thought, but proved a more formidable obstacle. This was Allah b. Zubayr (Zubayr, his father, was the Prophet's cousin). To his cause rallied the holy cities of Mecca and Medina, the Hejaz and southern Arabia, Iraq and part of Syria. Not until the reign of Abd al-Malik, third successor of Yazid, would this opposition be finally quelled, Mecca recaptured and the struggle against Byzantium resumed.

In spite of all this, from the moment Muawiya assumed power, the expansion of Islam went forward. These are the main lines it took. Eastward: 661, Herat, then the whole of Afghanistan, the Indus; this was followed by the occupation of Armenia; in 711, annexation of Transoxiana. Thus the threshold of China and India were reached. Westward: a victorious advance across North Africa; note the foundation of Kairawan by the Arab general Uqba, who used it as a base for his drive right to the Atlantic. To this mighty sweep from east to west, two well-known features belong: the defence of Carthage, its capture and pillage by the Arabs and its recapture by the Byzantines in 697; the resistance of the Berbers of Aurés under the leadership of Kahina, queen of a probably Judaized tribe, whose deeds became legendary. Quickly converted to Islam, the Berbers were a source of men and weapons for future conquests.

Then the pace of the cavalcades increases—southern Morocco, Tangiers, the Balearic Islands. From 711, under the impulse of Musa, governor of Ifriquiya (Tunisia) and his redeemed slave, Tariq, Spain was attacked and, in the space of seven years, all but totally conquered. The third successor of Musa crossed the Pyrenees in 717 or 718; the fourth seized Septimania and Narbonne which, for well-nigh a century and a half, remained a Muslim stronghold. The expedition against Toulouse failed in 721, but in the spring of 732 Bordeaux was taken and pillaged. And then on a Saturday in October 732 came the battle of Poitiers. Here the Muslim general, Abd al-Rahman, met his death and here, too, the Arab advances came to a halt. Not, though, their raids: Avignon taken in 734, Lyons pillaged in 743.

The Arab advance into Gaul never took on the appearance of anything but sallies. Narbonne was abandoned in 759 and the troops withdrew to Spain. But by that time the Umayyad Dynasty had ceased to rule at Damascus.

From 661, when Ali died, to 750, when the dynasty fell, fourteen caliphs had succeeded each other on the throne. This is the period usually known as the first Arab Empire. The Umayyads were descendants of the noble caravan merchants of Mecca and it was the Arab hegemony that they spread across the world. Contrary to the spirit of the Koran, the non-Arab converts to Islam remained *mawali*, "clients", a kind of second-class citizen. The Umayyad caliphs, with the exception of Umar II (717–20), a man of piety and sober living, are portrayed in history as having little concern for religious matters. Undoubtedly this accusation is open to amendment. But it is certain that they contributed to the downfall of the dynasty.

We may ask ourselves whether the great cavalcades of the Umayyad forces were really the outcome of the caliphs' urge for power, or whether we ought to link them with the great migrations of the nomadic tribes from the deserts to the fertile lands. Both explanations fit together. The Arab Muslim conquests were made possible by a complexity of ethnical, economic and political circumstances. And then, the historian, in analysing his facts, must bear in mind that these conquering armies found a great cohesive force in their enthusiasm for their new religion.

In any case, the Umayyads were gifted administrators. They were alive to the advantages of organizing and exploiting the conquered lands and to the wisdom of leaving undisturbed the framework of Byzantine administration. The process by which they turned their conquests to profit was a colonization of a religious, not a racial, pattern. The Christians and Jews were protected (*dhimmi*) in their person, their cult and their possessions. But they paid tax and their civic rights were, in some respects, limited. Conversions to Islam were often motivated by a desire to attain full rights of citizenship. This tendency was so marked that the central government had to restrain it, for fear the economic system of the State might collapse.

The accusation of religious laxity levelled against the Umayyads grew steadily. It was fostered by intense propaganda, which drew together the Shiite partisans, who demanded the reinstatement of the family of Ali, and the agents of the Abbasids. These latter were descendants of Ibn Abbas, uncle of the Prophet, remembered for fidelity to the pure Islamic observance. And they aspired to the throne. They had the advantage of the support of the *mawali*, non-Arab converts to Islam, who were often people with an ancient culture but were kept at a distance by the native pride of the Umayyad clan. A considerable number of the *mawali* were artisans and urban tradespeople. They rose against the Umayyads in the name of the right of all believers to full fraternity. Their intervention was to have important consequences.

Lack of unity among the Shiites also served the purpose of the Abbasids. The conflict between the white banner of the Umayyads and the black banner of the Abbasids is a famous page of history. It ended, in 750, with the proclamation of an Abbasid caliph, al-Saffah, in the mosque at Kufa and the defeat and massacre of the Umayyads. Out of them all only one, Abd al-Rahman b. Muawiya b. Hisham, managed to escape. He sought refuge in Palestine and later became the founder of the caliphate of Cordova.

The Abbasid dynasty lasted for five centuries, 750–1258.

Its capital was Baghdad. For a period it enjoyed brilliant heights of power but this was soon followed by a period of decline. The unity of the Muslim Empire was more than once in the balance.

ZENITH

In the course of the five centuries we have been examining, there were periods of widespread cultural influence, which left their mark on history far beyond the frontiers of the Muslim world. By and large, these periods coincide with times when the political power was at its highest, though they often outlived them. For example, there was Baghdad under Harun al-Rashid and his successors, from the end of the eighth to the tenth centuries. This was the epoch of the great translations from Greek and Syriac into Arabic, of the creation of the theological schools and the development of literature and art. Or again, at the other side of the Muslim world, Cordova in the tenth century and the beginning of the eleventh, the time of Hakam II and the poor scholar who became the famous vizier, Ibn Abi Amir al-Mansur. Then again with the tenth and eleventh centuries, the fame of Cairo of the Fatimids, with its great State University, al-Azhar, or the Aghlabid kingdom, whose influence was still felt in the court of Naples under Roger II and Frederick II. The ninth to the eleventh centuries were for Islam the golden age of humanist studies, which were to continue in Andalusia under the Berber dynasties of the Almoravids and Almohads.

PROTESTS OF THE PEOPLES (SHUUBIYYA)

The Arab Muslim culture of the courts spread gradually to the towns and the townspeople in their merchant and artisan corporations. But as this came about, there arose amongst the peoples of ancient cultures converted to Islam a consciousness of their own rights and potentialities, and these sentiments found expression in sporadic protests. This, amongst the non-Arab population, was particularly forceful on the part of the Iranians, in the east. It was in a way an echo of the *mawali* movement under the Umayyads, but of a more determinedly secessionist trend. Culture, religion and politics formed a single entity from which was to spring all the future history of Iran. There was also a perpetual alliance between Shia and the social protests of the people, and therein the Arabs and non-Arabs went hand in hand.

SOCIAL PROTESTS AND TRADE CORPORATIONS

A wide movement for social justice and equality was launched by Arab and Nabatean workers and, from the ninth to the twelfth centuries, spread in Khurasan, Syria and the Yemen. It even succeeded in bringing an independent State into being in Asha. This was the Quarmat movement, which nearly brought down the Abbasid Empire. Its organization comprised secret societies which were offshoots of the trade corporations, and in religious and political matters it adopted extremist Alid doctrines. The Fatimids took up the movement and harnessed it to their own objectives. Under the Fatimids, Cairo witnessed a great development of the trade corporations which played an effective part in political and social life. But because of their intimate association with Shia, there were initial difficulties with them when the Kurd Salah al-Din (Saladin) reconquered Egypt to Sunnism.

THE CRUSADES

The great historical event of the Crusades took place while the Abbasid dynasty was in power. One of their consequences was the establishment of the Frankish Kingdoms of Syria and Palestine—and the defeat of them both. The Crusades fall within the period 1095–1270. Details of them are not called for here. True enough, they were intimately linked with the political and religious affairs of the

West, but it should be noted that in Muslim history they do not assume the dimensions of events of lasting and primary importance. By the peoples of the Near East they are felt to have been unwarranted incursions by the Western powers and the forerunners of Western imperialism of later times. In the field of culture some Frankish traces were left behind, at least amongst the Christian communities of the East. But it was the Latin West that came under the influence of the Muslim East rather than the other way round.

The most significant outcome of the Crusades was really the reuniting of the Near and Middle East in Sunnite orthodoxy. This was brought about by the Kurdish general, the above-mentioned Sultan Salah al-Din. He belonged to the Abbasid family and was the Saladin of the tales of chivalry recorded in the Western chronicles and the favourite adversary of Richard Cœur de Lion and Philip Augustus during the Third Crusade. It was the defeat of the Frankish forces that made possible Saladin's reconquest of Egypt from their Fatimid allies. The fact that, a century after the Berber Almoravids had seized power in the Maghreb and at a time when another Berber dynasty, the Almohads, was about to succeed them, a Kurdish general was the champion of Sunnite orthodoxy, was the harbinger of the decline of the Arab hegemony, but by the same token it proves the universalism of Islam.

And indeed, in the face of all political and military vicissitudes, the Muslim way of life and Muslim religion, art, literature and science never ceased to flourish. "Foreign" influences—that is, non-Muslim—were certainly numerous and effective, especially that of classical Greece and, perhaps still more, the Persian epoch of the great kings. The princely patrons of the arts—the caliphs of Baghdad and the sultans (their not too loyal vassals) the caliphs of Cordova and the Berber dynasties—attained the dignity of an institution. The culture of Baghdad in the ninth and tenth centuries was more brilliant even than that of Byzantium, and Cordova was called the jewel of the universe. These princely patrons, it is true, were often very far from being an asset to the religious interests of Islam, and "free thinking", which commanded a considerable vogue, though it was periodically and violently attacked by the doctors of the Law, left the princes quite unconcerned. Yet never for a moment was there any thought of not belonging to the Muslim Community as such, and all these glories, however secularist, were retained as part and parcel of Muslim civilization.

THE MONGOL INVASION

Meanwhile new forces were restless on the frontiers. The great migrations from east to west continued. At the time of the Umayyads Islam had assimilated countless peoples by military expansion. But the Muslim Empire in its turn was invaded by the Turko-Mongols from the Iranian steppes. As early as the eleventh century, the Seljuk Turks, who had become Muslims, invaded Transoxiana and Khurasan, took possession of Persia and ravaged the Christian lands of Anatolia and Armenia. The Buyid viziers, who were Shiites, were in effect the rulers of Baghdad. The Seljuk Toghrul seized the town and made the caliph accept him as sultan. The Seljuk princes destroyed the preponderant influence of Iran throughout the Empire and declared themselves champions of strict orthodoxy. Their power, an essentially military one, was the forerunner of the Turko-Mongol conquests. At the end of the eleventh century their power was shaken by the Crusaders and, in the course of the next century, slowly crumbled away. At the beginning of the twelfth century another Turanian dynasty, the Khurasanians, brought about in Muslim Asia a brief triumph of Shia, whereas from 1171, a Kurdish Ayyubid dynasty was for a time the champion of Sunnite Islam.

And now there came to the threshhold of the Empire other Turanians from the deserts of Mongolia, who had precious little knowledge of Islam if any at all. The Kharezan domination crumbled under the blows of Genghis Khan who, at the beginning of the thirteenth century, conquered and pillaged Bactria, Afghanistan and Persia. Under the reign of his son, Ogatai, the Mongolian troops pushed forward to Vienna. The Crusaders had once tried to hit off an alliance with the Mongols against the Muslims and diplomatic relations were established between the papal court and that of the Mongols. Guyuk, successor of Ogotai and a Buddhist, took a kindly attitude towards the Armenian and Nestorian Christians. In 1251 he was succeeded by Mangu, son of a Christian princess, an educated man with religious insight and professing a broad syncretism. His brother, Hulagu, though a Buddhist, had a Christian mother and married a Christian himself. In 1258 he captured Baghdad. He massacred the Abbasid caliph and all his family but he let the Christians live.

Along with all this, the liberated slaves (Mamluk) had seized power in Egypt. One of the most famous of these, Baybar, took in an Abbasid who had escaped the massacre in Baghdad and had him proclaimed caliph in Cairo. The Mamluk dynasty continued to reign in Egypt and Syria, legitimized, as it were, by the establishment of this purely nominal caliphate.

To the extreme east, Kublilai, brother of Mangu his successor, had achieved the conquest of China, where he set up his empire. But the Mongols governing Persia became Islamized. Mongol troops clashed with those of the Mamluks. The former, commanded by a Christian, took Damascus in 1259. The last of the Crusaders hesitated to enter unreservedly into an alliance with them. In 1260 the Mamluk Sultan destroyed the enemy army near Nazareth and halted the Mongol advance. Less than half a century later, the Khan proclaimed Islam the State religion.

The Mongols, however, were never wholly Islamized. The successor of Hulagu remained a Buddhist and, like Hulagu, later married a Christian, the daughter of the Byzantine Emperor, Michael. Two centres of Muslim orthodoxy faced the Mongol powers. Starting in Anatolia, the Ottoman Turks under Bayazid I advanced into Asia Minor and conquered Bulgaria. But at the end of the fourteenth century, Timur-Lang appeared on the scene, a Turk and a Sunnite Muslim from Transoxiana, who had married two Chinese princesses. In three fast and furious cavalcades, swinging out from Samarkand, his capital, he ravaged Afghanistan, southern Russia and the north of India. And this he did in the name of the unity and orthodoxy of Islam. Then, turning on the Ottomans, men of his own religion, he vanquished Bayazid at the battle of Ankara. He died in A.D. 1405 (807 A.H.) toying with the idea of conquering China. The unity which Timur-Lang had striven to establish collapsed and his empire broke up into local principalities and dynasties, an easy prey in the never-ending wars.

The conquering Mongols had dreamt of a united empire but one which would no longer be a Muslim empire as such. The secularization of Islam came to an abrupt end. Timur-Lang wanted to rebuild Sunnite unity by force of arms. That failed also. This double failure held in itself the pattern of future efforts of this kind. The organization on a military pattern, which had assured the successes of the conquering Mongols and the Mamluk Sultans, was to be predominant, but the price paid would be the loss of cultural expansion. At the dawn of modern times, in the age of great discoveries, the route to India slipped from the hands of Islam and belonged to the Western maritime powers, and the Arabs and Arabized peoples ceased to hold sway over Muslim Asia.

Meanwhile, the Muslim West, that is, North Africa, had remained beyond the zone of Mongol invasions. During the fourteenth and fifteenth centuries, Hafsids ruled Ifriqiya, the Abd al-Wadites Tlemcen, and the Marinids were at Fez and a few places in Spain that had remained Muslim. It may be said that these three kingdoms foreshadowed the present-day Tunisia, Algeria and Morocco. In Spain, a small principality at Granada under the Nasrids endured in splendour until 1492.

THE MODERN AGE

The defeat of Bayazid I at Ankara was, for the Ottoman Turks, only a momentary eclipse. After the death of Timur-Lang, their military progress was resumed towards the west. Thus in 1453 Constantinople fell to Mohammed II. The importance of this date in European history needs no telling. It meant an end to the Byzantine Empire, the turning back of Greek culture on Italy and the dawn of the Western Renaissance.

From the sixteenth to the nineteenth centuries, four States between them shared the Muslim lands. The Ottoman Empire, which took Istanbul as its capital, reached its zenith under Selim I and Soliman the Magnificent, the ally of Francis I, whose troops besieged Vienna. This Empire had wrested Egypt from the Mamluks and had subjected North Africa, with the exception of Morocco which was able to retain its independence. It occupied Mesopotamia and Asia Minor and in Europe the Balkan Peninsula, Crimea and the islands of the Aegean. It became one of the pivots of European politics. Also, the Sultan of Constantinople had himself proclaimed caliph. But after the death of Soliman in 1566, the Empire stagnated, standing on the threshold of the West but never coming into it nor sharing in its technical achievements. Turkey was to become, in the unkind phrase, the "sick man" of nineteenth-century diplomacy. Its disintegration is spread across well nigh a century of European history: Greek independence, defeat in Crimea, occupation of Tunisia and Algeria by the French and of Egypt by Britain. The final assault came as a consequence of the 1914 war.

In addition, the Ottoman rulers had failed in their attempt

to rebuild Muslim unity in the East. Ismail, the founder of the Safawid dynasty, of Arab origin and a Shiite (Imamite), had conquered Iran (Persia) in 1501 and had himself proclaimed Emperor (Shah). Despite a costly defeat inflicted by the Ottoman Selim I at Tchaldiran in 1514, Persia under the Safawids held its own and even expanded somewhat towards the West. It achieved a brilliant period of culture and eventually established permanent relations with Europe. Two Persian monarchs, at least, earned fame, Shah Abbas (1557–1628) and Nadir Shah (1688–1747). Imamite Shia was implanted, not without fanaticism, by Shah Ismail, and even today it is still officially the State religion.

At the extreme east of the Muslim world, Baber (he died in 1530), a descendant of the Timurid Turcomans on his father's side and from the Genghis Khan on his mother's, seized Afghanistan, broke through into India and founded the Empire of the Great Moguls, which was to last until it became part of the British Empire. The last of the Great Moguls died in 1857. Their dynasty was, by religion, Sun nite Muslim. But the third sovereign, the famous Akbar (1542–1605), was attracted to Shia, adopted Persian as the official language in place of Arabic and, as a policy, welcomed Hindu influence. The dynasty soon returned to Muslim orthodoxy, witness the predominance of Sunnite adherence in the present-day Pakistan. Hindu Muslim syncretist influences were not eliminated for all that, and they have left their mark on many of the aspects of Indian Islam.

Sunnite orthodoxy was, then, maintained by the Ottoman Turks, the Turko-Mongols of India wavered between Sunnism and Shia, the Arab dynasty ruling in Persia professed Shia. At the extreme West was the fourth independent state, Morocco, the only country in North Africa to escape Ottoman dominion. Here, after the Marinids, came the dynasties of the Sherifs. They were Arabs and Sunnis, but just as much attached to the "family of the Prophet" as the Shiites were. Indeed they were descended from him through his grandson Hasan. The religious brotherhoods had a profound influence on the Berbers. The Sadian Sherifs ruled at Fez in the sixteenth and seventeenth centuries. The present dynasty there, the Alawids, are also Hasanid Sherifs and came to power in 1664. The diplomatic relations between Mawlay Ismail and France in the time of Louis XIV are well known. The independence of Morocco and its opposition to the Ottoman Empire and its link between the reigning sovereign and the "family of the Prophet" brought the sultan (later king) of Morocco the traditional title of imam, synonym of caliph. Thus, in Morocco, he is the chief of the believers, with the function of seeing that the politico-religious laws of the Koran are observed and of protecting the Community by armed force. Morocco is thus in the anomalous situation of having a "local" imam.

This modern epoch, which witnessed technical progress, an urge for conquest and also the slow dechristianization of the West, was a time of stagnation for Islam. Its social framework often became set in a feudalism of a more or less military kind, cultural development was paralysed by the slavish repetitions of manuals, commentaries and glosses on commentaries. But it would be utterly wrong to attribute this state of affairs to Islam itself: such a supposition is amply disproved by the brilliant achievements of the past under the Umayyads, the Abbasids and others.

It must be remembered, too, that the Muslim religion continued to expand geographically. There had been Muslim infiltrations in Madagascar from the seventh to the ninth centuries. Sumatra was Islamized in the thirteenth century. From the fourteenth century to the eighteenth, Islam gained Borneo and Celebes, increased its influence in China and got a foothold in Cambodia. It was found in Vietnam as early as the eleventh century. Its development in North Africa went on all the time. The Berbers had Islamized the western Sudan. Islam penetrated central Sudan in the fifteenth century and eastern Sudan soon afterwards. In the eighteenth century they were in "black" Africa, where there were then thirty to forty million Muslims.

THE CONTEMPORARY PERIOD

We do not intend to describe the evolution of the Muslim States at the present day. It is closely allied to European history. Four facts are here emphasized.

Firstly, during the nineteenth century the Muslim countries were faced with the colonial expansion of the European powers, while at the same time, the framework of the Ottoman administration remained intact in the Near East and so remained until the 1914 war gave it its death-blow. The Arab "revolt", and the part played by Lawrence of Arabia and Britain in connection with it, are well known. The Ottoman sultanate was suppressed in 1922 and the caliphate in 1924. Turkey, falling back on Anatolia and the region round Istanbul, set itself up as a secularist State. The Arabs or Arabized countries set about winning their independence, which was in some instances a rapid process and in others a slow one. So they found themselves little States, often with artificial boundaries. They constantly endeavoured to find some basis of union, even of unification. The league of Arab States, a supra-national body, was founded in 1945. It was not without its internal frictions on which the Western Powers kept a timely watch, and its practical efficiency was limited. But the creation of the State of Israel succeeded, in opposition to the league, in establishing a basis of unity, despite the Baghdad Pact in which figured Turkey, Britain, Iraq, Iran and Pakistan. Yet the centre of the stage seems to be held by Egypt, whose progressively successful bid for leadership of the Arab countries makes a strong appeal to the sentiment of the peoples concerned. February 1958 saw the proclamation and enthusiastic reception of the United Arab Republic (Syro-Egyptian), which the Yemen joined in the United Arab States. The Hashemite dynasties in Iraq and Jordan made an essay at federation in the Arab Union, but this collapsed with the revolt in Baghdad in July 1958, the assassination of King Faisal, and the establishment of the Iraqi Republic. Then also there was the declaration of independence in Tunisia and Morocco in 1956 and the upheavals in Algeria, all of which raised the hopes of Islam in North Africa for the effective unity of these three countries—the time-honoured Maghreb.

Secondly the importance of the great non-Arab groups, Pakistan and Indonesia, now independent States, must not be overlooked. The partition of India has had important political consequences and something like forty million Muslims live in the Indian Republic. But Pakistan (sixty-six million) and Indonesia (seventy million) are far and away the most populous of all Muslim countries. Whereas Indonesia is a secularist State, Pakistan declares itself an Islamic republic.

Thirdly the principal Muslim groups not forming States are now found in the U.S.S.R. (more than twenty-one million), in China ten million or more, and in the whole of "black" Africa together fifty-one to fifty-five million.

Lastly, the cultural reawakening, nothing short of a renaissance (*nahda*), sprang into being in the Arab countries of the Near East at the end of the nineteenth century, thus before they gained political independence. It is true that at first it was concerned with Arabic language and culture as such, and that it was the Christian Arabs who were responsible for it, but today it has assumed the form of a Muslim Arab revival. But the Muslims of Pakistan and Indonesia are not Arab-speaking peoples. Secularist Turkey and Iran, which is strictly Shiite, are developing a culture of their own. Then there is the U.S.S.R., which proclaims to the adherents of Islam that it favours national independence for all, while the industrial and economic efficiency of Marxist countries exercises an undeniable attraction on Muslim youth.

What will be the outcome? As educational facilities are

developed, whether in line with the Arab renaissance or as a result of a new-found consciousness of their native potentialities by the non-Arabic-speaking peoples, shall we see the common religious inheritance of Islam split up into separate national units, each a complexity of secular and religious elements, and undoubtedly courted by the far from Eastern dialectics of Marxism? Or shall we witness a new resurgence of Muslim culture, with the many languages and traditions working together on a common religious basis? And what eventually will be the part played by Arab nationalism, so very much alive today?

CHAPTER III

THE MUSLIM COMMUNITY

We have explained that Islam is at one and the same time and inseparably a religion, a legal and political entity and a culture.[1] The word used to convey this entity is *Ummat al-nabi*, the Community of the Prophet. An individual Muslim may be personally quite ignorant or even, as can happen nowadays, somewhat sceptical about Islam's traditional beliefs but for all that he will keep unimpaired the sense of fellowship with every other Muslim in the world and the sense of belonging to the Muslim body as a whole.

This word *umma*, community, is found in the Koran itself to designate the people of Islam and is derived from *umm*, mother. In modern usage it also designates "nation", in the

[1] We must be careful not to be too ready to read into this context Western notions derived directly or indirectly from Christianity. As Catholics we make the following distinctions: the Church "Christ continued", who has the words of eternal life; Christianity, the reflection of this truth lived in the hearts of the faithful; Christianity in its temporal aspect—the influence of the saints, all the spiritual exigencies encountered in everyday life, not to mention the burden of human weakness and inadequacy. This distinction is indispensable for a right understanding of the implications of the Christian Faith in the very mystery of the Church—a visible Church founded by Christ and preserved unaltered by the apostolic succession. But this has no parallel in Islam. The *dar al-Islam*, the house of Islam, the Islamic world, it cannot be overemphasized, is to be seen as a complex entity, political-juridical-religious. As Sheikh al-Maghari, Rector of the University of al-Azhar, said in 1939: "The celebrated distinction of render to God the things that are God's and to Caesar the things that are Caesar's has no meaning in Islam." Note that it follows that the Muslim "modernists", who endeavour to introduce this distinction, are at variance with the official doctrine.

Western meaning of the word. Thus *al-umma*, in the singular, means the Community of the Prophet and *al-ummam* in the plural is used of nations, such as Morocco, Iraq, Pakistan, etc. Other groups are at present in the course of formation. The Syro-Egyptian Republic is also called *umma*, while awaiting with often reiterated hopes a more extensive "Arab Nation", and it would seem that Tunis and Morocco would like to make a unit of countries covering the Maghreb.

Islam indeed presents two facets. If approached as one of the great religions of the world—and of course it is—it is usual to limit it to faith, dogma and canon law. In this way a cohesive pattern of thought and ideals is obtained. But if it is approached from the historical angle the easiest method seems to be to study each component part of the *dar al-Islam* individually and there is a great temptation to conclude that the Islam Community is the outcome of economic and political factors.

Nearly always in human history, however, we have to take into account many inter-related elements, and that is the case here. The religious element of Islam is and was a real influence. Mecca, the capital of caravan merchants, was in a sense ripe for monotheism. Yet there were many factors that militated in favour of tribal polytheism. Political and economic causes alone could not explain the creation of a supra-tribal community. For that we must look to Mohammed's religious intuition and his experiences: they gave the Community its orientation and, as time went by, the Community imposed a specific form of unity not only in matters of faith and dogma but even in the everyday way of life.

But if we revert to the other aspect, we find that it was indeed the economic and political and social conditions, first of Arabia and then of the Mediterranean basin and of more distant lands stretching away to the Indus, that made it possible for the Muslim Empires to develop and dominate, and with their triumph went the spread of Islam as a religion.[2] All this is so true that it may be said that opposite forces are at work though in different spheres throughout the history of the world of Islam—one making for uniformity, the other for diversity. It is with this double perspective in mind that we shall endeavour to define this political-religious Community, the *umma*.

MEMBERSHIP OF THE COMMUNITY

The native and common possession of the *umma* and its pre-eminent bond of union is a book, the Koran, looked on as the very word of God and, according to the most authoritative teaching, the *uncreated* word of God. It is tirelessly read and reread, learnt by heart, recited and meditated, digested and, with the magical fascination of its rhythmic prose, its admonitions, threats and promises, prescriptions and interdictions, it has sunk deep into the very texture of Muslim life.

This reverence for the Koran and the Arabic of its text offer a tentative basis for unity through a common language among Muslims throughout the world, whether Arabic-speaking or not.

From the earliest years the Community awoke to its own significance. It is the body (*jamaa*) of the believers, already foreshadowed by the group of Companions of Mohammed. The promise made by Mohammed is, "My Community will never come to agreement on error", and there is also the saying from a tradition of Ibn Abbas, "Whoever segrates himself from the Muslim body, be it only by the span of the hand, dies the death from before Islam". Such is the

[2] It would be all too easy to pretend to explain everything in retrospect by an underlying economic structure. For a balanced view of the question see the excellent work by W. Montgomery Watt, *Muhammad at Mecca*, quoted above, especially the chapter entitled "The Arabian Background".

principle of the *ijma*,[3] the consensus of all Muslims, or rather of those whose mission it is to represent them. Although it had no constitutional form, *ijma* was to become the highest criterion of orthodoxy. Membership of the *umma* is a guarantee for this world and the next. It is a *hukm*, a state, a juridical status, willed by God. One of the deepest sentiments derived from membership of *umma* is the certitude, not indeed of one's personal perfection, but of the perfection of the state of a believer in which one has been placed by God and which brings with it in this life the advantage of belonging to the "best possible people among men",[4] and, in the life to come, if one is faithful, the reward promised by the Lord.

A Muslim is any man who bears witness (*Shahada*) that "there is no God but God and Mohammed is his prophet". Or again, Muslims are the "people of the *qibla*", that is, those who turn in the direction of Mecca when they pray.

Aggregation to the Community is a simple matter. All that has to be done is to pronounce the *Shahada* and one belongs irrevocably to the *umma*. But this is something more than a mere verbal expression of faith; pronounced with heartfelt sincerity the *Shahada* is faith. For faith, *iman*, is to the Muslim essentially bearing witness—witness of the heart above all, to which is joined, unless it is completely impossible, witness of the tongue and members. The believer is a witness. That is why God bearing witness to himself in the Koran with the words, "I am God, there is no other God than me",[5] is really, in this technical sense, a "believer", *mumin*.[6]

What is more, the first part of the witness—"there is no

[3] The accepted Koranic basis of this ever since Shafii, is found in 4, 115: "He who shall follow another way than that of the believers, we accuse him of that with which he has accused himself. We shall bring him face to face with Gehenna. . . ." See below, concluding paragraphs of the present chapter.

[4] Koran, 31, 10.

[5] *Ibid.*, 20, 14.

[6] *Ibid.*, 59, 83.

God but God"—is sufficient in itself to ensure membership of the *umma.* Those words by themselves are indeed the *Shahada.* The acknowledgement of the mission of Mohammed, apostle of the oneness of God, follows as a matter of course. The deliberate and explicit denial of his mission would automatically annul the worth of the witness to God.[7]

What aggregation to the *umma* really does is to bring into actual being at a point in time a membership which, so Islam teaches, potentially belongs to all mankind. The formula of aggregation, the *Shahada,* so to speak, evokes the "pact", the great *mithaq,* of pre-eternity, granted by God to the human race on condition that it remains faithful in acknowledging him as its lord.[8] Membership of the Community becomes thus a kind of unfolding of the "pact", and the precepts of the Koran are the body of rules and guarantees liberally accorded by God to those whom he destines to be faithful to the "pact".

COMMON OBSERVANCES

By virtue of the *Shahada,* the explicit statement of the witness of faith, the life of a Muslim will be animated by a set of social and religious duties. Some of these are known as the "pillars of Islam"—prayer, legal alms, fasting and pilgrimage—and are a strict personal obligation. Others, such as the "struggle in the way of God" for the spread of Islam, are a duty of the Community but not of the individual

[7] Outside of Islam there is no salvation. The majority of doctors take this statement literally. They say that the only exception was for those people who, in pre-Islamic times, were faithful to a Prophet and a Law destined specially for them. There are, however, some thinkers like Ghazali, who believe in a kind of *in voto* membership of Islam: this would specifically be the situation of the "people of the Book" (Jews, Christians, Sabeans), who have received a revelation and a Law and are faithful to it but have never known Islam or, if they have, were kept from joining it by invincible prejudice through no fault of their own.

[8] Cf. Koran 7, 172.

believer. Others again which deal with man's relationship to his fellow men are sometimes obligatory and sometimes supererogatory, depending largely on circumstances of time and place. All these prescriptions taken together are what jurists usually call the "rights of God and of man". They are the true *shaair al-Islam*, the distinctive marks, the badge of Islam.

The four pillars of Islam

The pillars of Islam are usually defined as personal religious duties. It is however important to emphasize the sense of community which each of them imparts to Muslim life.

1. *The Friday prayer*. There are five daily prayers of obligation for the individual, but there is a duty of prayer for the Community as such in the midday prayer, the *zuhr*, each Friday. Wherever they may be at the time, if there is a sufficient number of them, Muslims are in principle obliged to recite this prayer together, grouped behind an *imam* and copying all his gestures.

2. *The duty of paying legal alms*. This is the *zahat* (poor tax) and amounts to a tenth or a fifth of one's income according to circumstances. It "purifies" the giver in regard to the increase of his possessions. It is an indispensable religious duty and many are indeed the texts which tell of the reward reserved in the future life for those who accomplish their alms deeds faithfully on earth.

But it is also a social duty, part of the machinery of the Community and so essential a part that no other tax must be exacted of the believer.[9] The *zahat* reminds the Muslim that he does not enjoy absolute free use of his possessions but that, in some measure, he must give an account of them

[9] In principle it fell to the "people of the Book" who were allowed to live among the Muslims to make up any deficiencies in the budget by payment of their taxes. Need we add that often in the course of history heads of State levied taxes (*mukus*) not prescribed by the Law.

to the Community, especially for the sake of the less fortunate of its members or to help forward works for the "rights of God."

3. *The ramadan, the fast which lasts a lunar month.* This is not merely a personal but also a public affair. Once again, here is a religious act of obligation for the individual and one which is only pleasing to God and recompensed by him in the future life if it complies with the strict regulations set down for its accomplishment. But the rigid details of the fast, kept from sunrise to sunset, are the immediate concern of the city, whose business it is to supervise their observance.[10] It is quite certain that the *ramadan* stimulates in the fasting Muslim the true mentality of Islam, the sense of belonging to the people of Mohammed. The festival which closes the month's fasting (known as the *fitr*) ranks second in the great festivals of the Muslim year.

4. *The pilgrimage to Mecca.* This is of foremost significance as a manifestation of common life. It is known as the *hajj*. Every believer who is able to do so must make this pilgrimage at least once in a lifetime. On the appointed days each year, at the foot of the desert hills where no non-Muslim may enter under pain of death, there is experienced, as it were, the presence of the entire Muslim Community. The colourful variety of races and peoples seems to merge into one uniform pattern and the sacred state into which each pilgrim enters is as it were the highest fulfilment of the status of believer. From the instant the ancient and beautiful cry of *labbayka* ("Behold me for thee, O God") goes up, the pilgrim has but to let himself be carried on the rushing waves of the ancient ceremonies that have withstood the centuries as the symbol and rallying call of the Community.[11] Then comes the procession seven times round the Kaaba, the "house of God", which was rebuilt by Abraham with the

[10] Eating, drinking, smoking, etc. in public is forbidden.

[11] Cf. John Abdel-Jalil, *Aspects intérieurs de l'Islam*, Ed. du Seuil (Paris 1949), pp. 117–27, for some beautiful prayers of the pilgrimage.

help of his sons, says the Koran,[12] and where the black stone of the ancient cults is still enshrined and venerated. Then come the seven "races" between the hillocks Safa and Marwa, in memory of Hagar who, when she was repudiated, ran to seek water to quench the thirst of her son Ismael. Then the halts at the sanctuaries around Mecca and the hurried walk from one to the other, the halt at Mount Arafat which is the culminating point of the pilgrimage, the stoning of the demon in the Valley of Mina, the slaughtering of the animals offered in memory of the sacrifice of Abraham, the offering of hair; the pace gains momentum at every instant and the crowds surge with one great and collective enthusiasm, the union of each and all brought home still more by the fact that all, king or beggar, wear absolutely an identical garment, the sacred *ihram*. Maimonid taught that the *hajj* had a sacrificial value from which the whole Muslim Community benefited. Each year, on the days assigned for the sacrifices of the pilgrimage, sheep are killed throughout the Muslim world in union with the pilgrims. This is known as the "great festival", the "festival of sacrifice". But these local celebrations only have a religious value because they are a participation in the sacrifices at Mecca and a commemoration of them.

The duties of the Community

1. *The fight in the way of God* (*jihad*). There is a tendency to express this in European languages as "the holy war". This is what it really means: the Community must, at some point or other in its territories, keep up the struggle for the extension throughout the world of the "rights of God and of man" laid down in the Koran. The Muslim Brotherhood, it is true, holds that the duty of furthering this by armed force still exists, but most contemporary reformers teach that the obligation can be fulfilled by the peaceful means of missionary work, the *dawa*. When, however, a Muslim country is attacked, the duty becomes an individual one and every

[12] 2, 127.

Muslim, even women and children if they are able, is bound to answer the call to arms.

Jihad means exertion, effort, in the way of God. It does not imply general extermination in the sense of *khorban* in the Bible. Laws regarding *jihad* were promulgated during the time of the Abbasid Empire stipulating, among other things, that only enemy combatants taken with weapons in their hands could be killed immediately. The passages of the Koran on which the laws of *jihad* are based are susceptible of other interpretations. There is no reason why they should not incorporate the present-day requirements of international law.

2. *Offices of the Community*. These are political-religious or juridical-religious offices. The principal ones are: caliph or supreme imam, the guide of the Community; the *qadi* or judge, whose judgements are based on the principles of the Koran, the *mufti*, the *prudens*, who is the jurisconsult; the *muhtasib*, whose task is to ensure honesty in commercial transactions; the *udul*, who are qualified witnesses and, along with the *mufti*, also act as notaries. There are various requirements for appointment to each of these offices but one qualification is always demanded, or is supposed to be, namely, *adala*, equity, which means moral and canonical conformity to the laws of the Koran. For the *dar al-Islam* only deserves its name if it is also truly *dar al-adl*, the land, the world of justice.

The exercise of these offices is the responsibility of the Community, whose duty it is of seeing that they are entrusted to competent men. If it happens that in any given locality there is only one man with the requisite qualifications then he is under an obligation to accept office.

3. *Everyday life*. Many other prescriptions, some obligatory some not, are woven into the life of every Muslim from the cradle to the grave. There are the ritual prayers which, even though they may be said privately, are accompanied with carefully prescribed gestures and attitudes. There is the

adhan, the call to prayer five times each day shouted by the muezzin from high up in the minaret. There are the legal requirements for the purification ablutions and the faithful following of the lunar calendar. Then there are the canonical regulations concerning marriage, the pattern of family life, the laws regarding inheritance,[13] cemeteries belonging to the Community for the exclusive use of Muslims and which must never be alienated, the distinctions between licit and illicit meat, the special regulations for the slaughter of licit animals —so that even in the matter of food one is made conscious of belonging to the Community. There is, too, the ban on alcoholic drink, gambling and usury, and there is the "obligatory custom", traditional, though not laid down in the Koran, of circumcision, often popularly though wrongly looked on as the initiation ceremony of Islam.

We must also point out the institution of the *waqf* or *habus*, property made over to God and the revenue from it used for pious works or public utility. As time went on, this system gave rise to many abuses, especially in the matter of "private *waqf*", which made over the usufruct of real estate to individual beneficiaries. Modern Muslim States tend to include in their proposed amendments the revision of the laws regarding *waqf* and the suppression of private *waqf* altogether. What must be emphasized is that the idea of *waqf* does show that the pious Muslim is encouraged to make a willing surrender of his possessions.

The wearing of the face veil by women and their exclusion from social life was for a long time looked on as one of the characteristics of the Muslim way of life. At the present time there is a decisive move towards opening up public life to women.

Coming to grips with the ever-growing need for present-

[13] Female heirs are the foremost example of heirs who cannot be disinherited, but they have right to only half as much as a corresponding male heir.

day technical developments, the enlightened Muslim reformers endeavour to establish two categories of practices in the Community life of Islam. On the one hand are certain indispensable practices, everything that has come down directly from the teaching of the Koran or the undisputed traditions of Mohammed. These Islam cannot renounce without being false to itself. On the other hand, there is the accumulation, sometimes a complex one, of customs grafted on to Islam but belonging to outmoded states of culture. These the Muslim countries must alter if they are to survive and develop in the world today.

But there is a more searching distinction to be made within the text of the Koran itself—all of which, it must be remembered, the Muslims believe to have been dictated by God—a distinction between the beliefs and mode of worship, on one hand (*aqidat* and *ibadat*), which are sacrosanct and, on the other, moral precepts (*akhlaq*), which are open to adaptation and, especially, social relations (*muamalat*) which can vary to suit circumstances of time and place. Thus, with the texts as a starting-point, new legal formulas could be progressively elaborated. This distinction was mentioned long ago by Abu Hamid al-Ghazali, known in medieval Europe as Algazel, and given prominence in the fourteenth century by the great Hanbalite, Ibn Taymiyya. Contemporary reformers quote them as their authorities.

It would seem, then, that the Muslim States are faced with this alternative: will they take the initiative in conducting the development now afoot in a manner that will keep it within the spirit of the Muslim faith; or, will they wait until secularization is a *fait accompli* and then step in to ratify it with an adaptation of Koranic law? In the final analysis, the problem amounts to a searching of the Muslim conscience in the face of the present-day technical advances and the constant appeal of modern efficiency. The matter is referred to again.

COMMUNITIES AND INTERMEDIARY GROUPS

There can be no doubt that the Muslim Community presents itself as a universalism, making no distinction between person, race or class. "The believers are brethren," says the Koran,[14] and a frequently quoted tradition from Mohammed says: "Men are all equal like the teeth of a weaver's card. There is no distinction between white and black, Arab or non-Arab, except in the measure in which they fear God." And yet if we look at the detailed history of the Muslim Community down the centuries, we shall find that its striking characteristic is the impetus it derived from the *peculiarities* of tribes, or races, nations and economic conditions. Let us examine each of these elements.

The tribes

The first political-social organization encountered by Islam was the tribe. It was also the first it set itself to conquer. The spiritual bond of the Muslim faith was supra-tribal: it was this that so profoundly revolutionized pre-Islam Arabia. In point of fact, the economic requirements of Mecca, the great inter-tribal caravan centre, lent itself to this change. The ground was prepared for the moulding together of the tribes and thus also for the suppression of local deities in favour of a One and Only God. It remains true that the pact of the Sahifa, established by the Prophet between the Meccans and the people of Medina, was a pact of brotherhood, transcending blood relationships, for it was based on the higher principle of submission (Islam) to the will of God.

But the mass of believers who gained entry into the *umma* kept their former ties and hatreds: there was no particular reason to forgo them. It was a stroke of political genius on the part of the first caliph when he gave this supra-tribal organization, still as yet fragile, a common enemy to fight, namely, the infidels who still held out against Islam.

[14] 49, 10.

But wherever their triumphant cavalcades landed them, these conquering Arabs were torn by intestine quarrels—whether in Iraq or in Andalusia, one way or another, everything that befell them can be explained by the story of the tribes.

Anyone who looks at the progressive Muslim conquests from the point of view of the theologian and jurist of Islam would be tempted to explain them in terms of a unity inspired by the new faith. But anyone who looks at them as a modern historian does, with an eye for the relationship between successive events and their interaction, will be tempted to explain everything, or almost everything, by tribal friction stimulated by faith in God and an urge for conquest growing in magnitude as it spread out from the Arabian peninsula to the very limits of the known world. Both these approaches are valid.

In point of fact, the supra-tribal cohesion of Islam lent itself admirably to the survival of the tribes themselves and their *esprit de corps* (*asabiyya*). Ibn Khaldun studies them in the fourteenth century. Even from the religious point of view there was perpetuated the tradition of one tribe being privileged among all others, namely, the Quraysh, because the Prophet belonged to it. It was directly the Koranic faith that brought the tribal bonds slowly to extinction; that was done by the great bodies of ancient civilizations conquered by Islam and later, in modern history, by the creation of the States and nations which tended to replace the ties of blood with a sense of belonging to a particular land and sharing a common destiny in history.

Ethnical groups

Stronger still was the ambivalence in the specifically racial sphere, at least in the case of the Arabs. Even though tribal ties of blood might be forgotten, pride in belonging to the Arab people was still vindicated.

We have already spoken of the Arab Empire of the Umayyads and the protest of the *mawali*, the non-Arab "clients", with the ultimate revolt of the peoples (*shuubiyya*). There will be constant clashes between Islamic universalist principles and the vindication of Arab supremacy. It is noteworthy that wherever ethnical Arab minorities settled, Islamization and Arabization went hand in hand. Today the Copts of Egypt and the Berbers of Maghreb proudly declare that they are Arabs. In the governmental sphere, the political power of the Arab League was halted by internal dissensions, while the ideal of the "Arab nation" gave rise to boundless enthusiasm. What is more, with Muslims who have become thoroughly secularist in outlook and culture, the pride of belonging to the Arab people remains as a last link holding them still to the Faith of the Prophet.

Non-Arab racialism is unthinkable in Islam. It would mean an immediate break with the *umma* and immediate rejection by it. The attempts at "Turanianism" were a clear sign of that. An exaltation of the destiny of the Arabs, even if it went beyond the limits of the one permissible sphere of adulation, would in fact serve to foster Muslim cohesion. There is, however, one possible exception, namely, the case of the Arab or Arabized Christians. Recently they have awakened to the fact that their culture, their past and their outlook for the future are Arab. This may call for a new historical perspective, by virtue of which two distinct spheres in the *umma* would be acknowledged: in the religious sphere, a complete and universal fraternity with non-Arab Muslims; in the temporal sphere, a real fraternity with non-Muslim Arabs arising from a consciousness of a common destiny in history. How far this might go would depend on the amount of effective liberty allowed to the Arab Christians, and the measure in which they would be allowed to hold office in the administrative machinery of the new Arab nations—or will it be a new Arab *Nation*?

The nations

The modern age stresses national sentiment. It is a sentiment that came late to the Muslim Community. In countries that have long since enjoyed autonomy it is keenly felt but in other regions it does not seem to have made much impact on the lives of the people. The way some of the Arab territories were parcelled out after the 1914 war was purely arbitrary. The natural process is for the machinery of the State to develop from within a nation but, instead of that, the State machine was set up ready-made and the nation was expected to grow out of it. The problem, however, is different when it comes to countries that were formerly colonies or protectorates; for there the idea of nationhood is consolidated by the enthusiasm of the people in their struggle for independence. Nor does the problem exist in countries that have long been independent. Sometimes, especially among peoples of a set existence from remote times, the idea of the nation will be predominant, sometimes it will be purely and simply identified with race consciousness, but still more often race consciousness will tend to merge various national groups into one larger unit, in which nationality and race become indistinguishable. The clearest example of this is to be found in the present political evolution in Egypt.

By and large, the process of evolution from the tribe to the nation by way of racial consciousness (or conjointly with it) seems to be a well-known phenomenon in history and not one specifically linked with Islam. Islam's propensity for stamping everything in the temporal sphere with its own pattern will have to give way to a more subtle and more comprehensive approach. Thus in its own interests it will have to ensure access to full rights of citizenship for the non-Muslim minorities, for the Rights of Man stipulated by international law would never countenance nowadays the status of *dhimmi*, a kind of second-class citizen, to which the Umayyads and Abbasids subjected these minorities.

Economic groups

But the age of self-sufficing national groups is a thing of the past and its place has been taken by large political-economic groups. The unity that belongs specifically to the *umma* is of a political-religious kind. Will it be able to command a sufficient cohesion to constitute a firm group in the sphere of temporalities, capable of holding its own in relation to the great powers whose strength lies especially in their economic structure?

From its very beginnings and especially from the time the Umayyads came to power, in the sphere of economics Islam turned to good account the lands it had conquered. It entrusted its high finance to "tributaries", who were Jewish or Christian, but Jewish for preference, and at the same time launched the employment of "colonial" labour for the workshops in the towns and for agricultural projects. Muslim civilization proper proved to be essentially urban, establishing its centres in the rich valleys or in the peripheral regions backing on the vast central deserts. Thus it needed to have control of the seas and the coastal routes. These Islam lost first as a result of the development of the Portuguese navy and later of that of Holland and Britain. What is more, it lost the land route to India. Thus Islamic territory was left with no outlet. This happened at the very time when the power of the military oligarchy of the Turko-Mongols was gaining ascendancy. The twofold stagnation, economic and cultural, of the Islamic lands coincided with the modern age when the Western powers threw themselves headlong into policies of aggrandizement and material gain.

But for some decades now, there is evidence of a steady recovery. With very few exceptions the Islamic territories still rank as underdeveloped countries. The extraordinary mineral wealth in certain regions (petroleum, tin, phosphates, etc.), the remarkable quality of their agricultural products and cattle breeding and, in addition, the determined will of the people to bring themselves up to a standard of living that will warrant their freedom and enable them to recapture their past splendour, all this makes of the Muslim body an element that must be increasingly reckoned with in the balance of world affairs.

The isolationist tendency of national units in modern times has served to emphasize the economic weakness of each separate Muslim State. The excessive division of the Middle East into small units after the 1914 war brings out this weakness still more and the political independence of these States, achieved with such great difficulty, runs the risk of being paid for at the price of economic subjection to one or another of the great powers. The determination to escape such subjection at all costs dominates present-day policy of the Arab world. So keenly do the people feel about this that it would be folly not to take it into account.

The religious unity of the Muslim world is closely rooted in its temporal interests. That unity, it would seem, can only survive at the present day if it provides itself with an adequate economic basis. This seems to be the crux of the problem.

CHAPTER IV

SOURCES AND FORMULATION OF BELIEF

During the first centuries of Islam there were several forms of "profession of faith". They all had a common basis but varied from school to school and gained in clarity in the face of doubt and denials. Through all its temporal vicissitudes, the Muslim Community always lived by its beliefs (*aquidat*). It will be well to give here a brief account of their evolution and content.

It is safe to say that the chief dogmas of Islam are: the Oneness of God, the word of God communicated to man by the Prophets and their Books, the resurrection of man and the last judgement, the rewards and punishments of the future life, the existence of angels and predestination.

We shall return to these at the end of this chapter. But at the outset it must be noted that very early the *ulum al-din*, that is, the religious sciences or religious knowledge, in which dogma and law are intimately related, began to be studied. This brought to the fore the problem of method and sources.

THE SOURCES

There are four main sources of religious science.

The Koran

This, as we have said, is the common possession of the whole Muslim Community and its great bond. By the same token, it is the supreme body of law, *shar*, where the believer learns the content of his faith but also his rule of life: for the Koran is *al-furqan*, the "distinction", between good and evil. The fusion of the temporal and the spiritual, so characteristic of Islam, makes of the Koran at one and the same time the code of ethics for the individual and for society and the structure of the commonwealth. Thus the Koran is the primary source of dogma, morals and jurisprudence.

The hadith

A second source consists of the corpus of *hadith*. These are sayings and actions attributed to the Prophet (Mohammed), preserved by a proven chain of reliable "transmitters", starting with one or more of the Companions of Mohammed who handed on by word of mouth what they had heard and witnessed. It is generally believed that when Mohammed had to take a decision he was prophetically inspired, except when he himself said that he was just giving his personal opinion (*ray*). Thus, in the eyes of Muslim tradition, the *hadith*, provided they are shown to be genuine, enjoy that authority of revelation. It may happen that some particular *hadith* throws light on the Koranic text itself, sometimes even correcting it. The jurists readily assert that the example of the Prophet, thus guaranteed, has force of law. The corpus of the *hadith* is called *sunnat al-nabi*, the practice of the Prophet, or simply, Sunna.

Qiyas

It may happen, however, that circumstances arise which are provided for in neither the Koran nor the Sunna. The procedure then is to take a text which deals with a similar situation and formulate a judgement by analogy; in this way the solution can be said to have a foundation in the "writings". This argument from analogy is called *qiyas*. It is looked on as the third source of Muslim law and religious science.

Ijma

The fourth source is the *ijma*. We have already stressed its importance in speaking of membership of the Community in the previous chapter. It consists in the consensus of the Muslim Community, which would never "agree on an error". The consensus of the Companions of the Prophet is unassailable and universally accepted. But most schools of thought have accepted as *ijma* the consensus of the doctors of a given period, provided their findings have a basis in the text of the Koran or at least that they are not at variance with any text of Islamic writ. The notion of *ijma* is fundamental. It is true that *ijma* as such has never been constituted as a juridical corpus. Besides, alongside the notion of explicit *ijma* as the consensus of a sufficient number of doctors—in principle unalterable—there is the notion of tacit *ijma*, implicit in any established traditional custom that is not at variance with the Koran or Sunna. But an explicit *ijma* can always invalidate an implicit one. The organization of *ijma* is the main hope of present-day Muslim reformers.

There, then, are the four fundamental sources: the Koran, the Sunna, *qiyas* and *ijma*. But there are also secondary sources. They serve to amplify and even to supplement argument by analogy, but always in subservience to *ijma*: thus, the personal interpretation of a doctor, the welfare of the commonwealth, pre-Islamic or non-Islamic usage wherever it was not in contradiction with the "writings". This last is known as *urf* (general usage, customary law) and it played a considerable rôle in the history of the law. The recognized schools of law were to owe their individual characteristics to their definitions of *qiyas* and *ijma* and the degree of importance they attached to the secondary sources.

The study of the sources belongs to a special branch of learning which is linked with Canon Law. It is an indispensable requisite for the Muslim who studies any aspect of religious science. Or, to put it another way, the sources from which law has been elaborated, *usul al-fiqh*, are at the same time authentic theological sources. They are part and parcel of what are called the sources of religion (*usul al-din*). The branch of learning usually known as Muslim theology is not so much theology in the strict sense of the word as apologetics: the defence of beliefs against those who deny or doubt, a science that harks back to the sources every bit as much as do the legal studies.

All religious studies use the same method: research, the student's individual effort, *ijtihad*, as he works on texts and scrutinizes the sources. Now, in Islam there is no living magisterium in doctrinal matters. The supreme imam or caliph is the temporal head of the Muslim Community, entrusted with the administration of the juridico-religious law of the Koran and the Sunna. It is not for him to define dogmas. Only the *ijma* might exercise that power, but, as we have seen, it has never been set up as a constituted body, and its very definition varies from one school of thought to another. The only criterion of orthodoxy, therefore, is the Koran or the Sunna.

In such conditions as these, the principle of personal research carried with it a danger: it could involve the Community in a babel of contradictory interpretations. Quite early on, schools of thought on religious matters came into being. In the ensuing controversies, which were sometimes of considerable violence, some schools were driven out of existence, others gained favour and for centuries were looked on as the embodiment of orthodoxy, though they were never given official status in that respect. From as early as the third and fourth centuries A.H., personal research could only be carried on within the limits imposed by accepted schools of thought. Furthermore, the discipline determining everyday observances and social relations, namely, Canon Law (*fiqh*), became fixed in manuals of jurisprudence. Thus was brought about the "closing of the door on personal research", a measure which soon spread to other branches of studies. From the fourteenth and fifteenth centuries A.D. commentaries and glosses fettered Muslim thought, at least that of Sunnism, which was then predominant.

As early as the thirteenth–fourteenth centuries, the great Ibn Taymiyya demanded the reopening of the "doors of personal research and opinion" and all reformers have done likewise. Present-day reformers, those who hope to give *ijma* (consensus of doctors, etc.) an effective constituted form, consider this demand indispensable for any revival in Islam. To their way of thinking, it would be the Muslim answer to present-day needs. It would, they say, offer an opportunity for new scope and method and it would arrest the secularization of social principles which is constantly gaining ground.

RELIGIOUS SCIENCES

It would be out of the question to give here a detailed history of each branch of religious studies. A brief survey must suffice.

Exegesis

From its infancy Islam held the study of religion in high esteem. At first, during the Medina period, it would seem to have taken the form of *reading* the Koran, to which was soon added exegesis or interpretation, *tafsir*.

Koranic exegesis is based on the notion that revelation is all of a piece. That is, it is not *inspired*, in the sense in which Catholic theology uses that word, but God *revealed* every word of it to Mohammed through an angelic messenger. Hence the task of the exegete is to study the text itself with a view to grasping what God ("he who speaks") wished to express. The approved method of exegesis is twofold: first the exegete must have a thorough grasp of the usage of the Arab tongue at the time of Mohammed, secondly, he must be able to reconstruct the historical circumstances in which the various verses (*Suras*) of the Koran "came down from heaven". Hence the prime importance of grammar and syntax and the wide use made of Arab pre-Islamic traditions and details of the daily life of the Prophet and his Companions at Mecca and Medina.

Given the Islamic notion of revelation, the study of literary sources does not arise. The only "source" is God's uncreated word. At the very most, the exegetes will make use, some liberally others with great caution, of Christian and, still more, Jewish traditions. But these are considered not as possible origins of the Koran but as kindred documentation which may prove helpful, for example in throwing light on the history of the prophets.

The two most famous names in Koranic exegesis are Tabari (died 922) and Zamakhshari (1074–1144), who went so far as to use "arguments from reason". The work of these two was freely quarried by later commentators. Thus, Fakhr al-Din, al-Razi, Baydawi, Jalalayn. Many of these exegetes were also theologians, and the way they interpret texts is often linked with the particular school of theological thought to which they belong. In recent times, the most strongly "rationalist" exegesis (that is, proceeding by arguments from reason), the *salafiyya*, endeavoured to harmonize Islam and modern thought, though in reality they left the Muslim notion of revelation unaltered. The only attempt ever made to alter that was the recent study of Mohammed Ahmad Khalafallah, a doctor of the University of Cairo. What he suggests is the application of the principles of literary form to the study of the Koran. His thesis, which he defended in 1947, provoked the opposition of al-Azhar and violent controversies on the subject went on for several years. It can hardly be said that his views have been accepted.

Hadith

The study of the Sunna of the Prophet gave rise to the science of *hadith*. This must not be thought of as a commentary or an historical study of the text itself of the traditions:

it only deals with the external critique of the chains of transmitters. The solidity of the chain or the fact that a given text is supported by one or several chains, determines the value to be attached to a *hadith*. Only a "genuine" *hadith* is unassailable. It is permissible, however, to take into account a "good" *hadith*, whereas a "weak" *hadith* is worthless as an argument from authority. A *hadith mursal* and a *hadith qudsi*, traced back to a prophet other than Mohammed or to a direct revelation from God, fall into a special category, at any rate in the study of mysticism.

A lengthy study was undertaken to sort out the innumerable *hadith* in circulation. The outcome of this was that, in the third century A.H. (ninth and tenth century A.D.) six corpus of *hadith* were compiled by Bukhari, Muslim, Ibn Maja, Abu Dewud, Tirmidhi and Nashai. The first two, especially that of Bukhari, enjoy unchallenged authority.

In each corpus the *hadith* are classified according to their contents: faith, the Pillars of Islam, the details of religious worship or actions related to it (as for instance the ritual ablutions), the Last Ends, social relations, the branches of law—all are provided with innumerable prescriptions and elucidations. There is still a vast amount of research to be done in this field.

Law (*fiqh*)

The original meaning of *fiqh* was "reflection". It was later used to designate roughly speaking what we call Canon Law. We have already spoken of the capital importance attached to it in Muslim life and thought. Its beginnings are found at an early date at Medina. It took definite shape through the work of four great jurists who gave their names to four celebrated legal schools, all of them equally orthodox. It should be noted that there are sometimes notable differences between the views of the founders of these schools and the solutions put forward later by those claiming to belong to them. One of these four pioneers, Ibn Hanbal, was a traditionalist—a doctor in the science of traditions, *hadith*, rather than a jurist.

The *fiqh* includes two sections: the sources or foundations, which partly coincide with the "sources" of religion, and the "branches", which deal with the legal requirements for prayer and ablutions, as well as with all kinds of contracts, marriages, wills, sale of property, etc.—the entire framework of the round of daily life.

Recent works stress the evolution and constitution of Muslim jurisprudence from the historical angle, closely related as it was to many economic and political issues and constantly influenced by them. It is all the more regrettable that such developments should have been so long halted by the rigidity of the manuals of jurisprudence. At any rate, it can be said that the four great legal schools were, in all essentials, established by the end of the third century A.H. (ninth century A.D.). They are still extant today. Here are their founders and their main characteristics:

1. Malik Ibn Anas (died at Medina, 795). From him came the Malikite school or rite. He attaches great importance to the *hadith* but supplements tradition with the practice of the Community at Medina and the consensus of its doctors. When he thinks fit, however, he amends tradition in the light of the principle of the welfare of the commonwealth (*maslaha, istilah*). Thus, within certain limits, personal opinion (*ray*) is invoked. This school is today prevalent in the Maghreb (Tunisia, Algeria, Morocco).

2. Abu Hanifa. An Iranian who taught in Iraq (died 767). He is the founder of the Hanafite school. This school is usually considered the broadest of all legal schools. It is certainly true that it is prepared to make good use of reason. Thus it gives preponderance not only to personal opinion (*ray*) but also to the preferential judgement (*istihsan*) of the prudent man, and above all, makes use with considerable liberty of the third source of law, *qiyas* or argument from analogy. From the very first this school accepted a form of

reasoning by which argument from like to like is, in certain conditions, conclusive. We can say that without going so far as the clear notion of the universal middle term, the Hanafite *qiyas* is the forerunner of the Aristotelian *qiyas—syllogism*, which was soon to be taught in the formal logic of the great mosques. The Hanafite school spread throughout the East under the Seljuks, and was the official rite of the Ottoman Empire. At the present time it is predominant in Turkey. It is found as a rival to the Malikite and Shafiite schools in the countries formerly under the rule of Istanbul.

3. Shafii, an Arab of the Quraysh tribe, died in Egypt in 820. He founded the Shafiite school. Unlike Abu Hanif and Malik, he rejected the use of personal opinion of the prudent together with the argument from the welfare of the commonwealth. He emphasizes consensus (*ijma*). Malik invoked consensus of the doctors of Medina. Shafii extended the notion of *ijma* to mean the consensus of the doctors of a given epoch, thus making *ijma* an inexhaustible source of elucidation. This consensus, taken in reference to the text of the Koran and the Sunna, provides both the starting point and the material for argument by analogy.

4. Ibn Hanbal, born of an Arab family. Died at Baghdad, 855. He is the author of the famous collection of traditions called *Musnad*. The Hanbalite school of law was not founded by him but by his disciples, who drew their inspiration from his teaching. This school is looked on as specially rigorist, because of its opposition to all *bida*, "innovation", and for its constant reference to the texts of the Koran and the Sunna alone. Thanks to this, the Hanbalites were often led to take as authentic *hadith* (traditions) not accepted by other schools. In the eighteenth century, Hanbalism was vigorously championed by the Wahhabite reform as the only authentic doctrine, and today it is the official rite of Saudi Arabia. And, indeed, its importance far outreaches the feudal dependences of the Najd. It had its rise under the aegis of the great Ibn Hanbal, of sincere and deeply interior piety, and

before it was supplanted by Hanafism in Syria and Iraq, it produced many a current of sound, pious living and even created an atmosphere of genuine popular piety. In its basic principles it uses the utmost rigidity. The only *ijma* (consensus) it admits is that of the Companions of the Prophet. But at the point where *ijma* is brought to a close, the greatest of the Hanbalites, for instance Ibn Taymiyya, show a readiness to make use of personal research (*ijtihad*) and a preoccupation with saving the spirit rather than the letter. It is not by mere chance that the present-day reformers, endeavouring to adapt Islam to the modern world, turn primarily to the Hanbalite traditions. But they do not stop there —and it may be that their line of thought, should it become generally accepted, would be the means of revitalizing the science of *fiqh* (jurisprudence). Some reformers, indeed, would like to see modern Muslim jurists work out which laws would offer a common ground to the four "orthodox" schools. Some even go so far as to invite the Shiites of varying shades of opinion to join this new form of Muslim rite.

Kalam (*apologetics*)

This is the fourth and last branch of religious science in the strict meaning of the term. Its meaning varies—science of the oneness of God (*ilm al-tawhid*), science of speech about God (*ilm al-kalam*), approximately, one might say, Muslim theology. The following are its principal schools or trends:

1. Three trends are found under the Umayyads: (a) The Murjiites, who held that no fault committed by a believer could be a grave fault and left to the merciful decision of God the eternal fate of a believer who sinned. (b) Khadarites, who held that man enjoyed absolute freedom of action and that he was the creator of his own acts. (c) Jabarites, who held that because the omnipotence of God is absolute, man is in his regard an automaton.

2. The first "school" worthy of the name, or rather the first group of them, is represented by the Mutazilite trends.

At first—in the first century A.H.—the Mutazila were concerned with politics: it was the time when the legal position of the caliphate was being fought out. But in the second and third centuries, they turned their attention to doctrine. We may look on them as the continuators of the Khadarites, for like them, though with some slight modifications, they were the champions of man's freewill. For them, reason is the criterion of the law and the revealed word presented in the form of a book—Torah, Gospel, Koran—is a *created* thing, by contrast with the orthodox Muslim notion of an eternally existing text communicated all of a piece to man. They styled themselves the "Champions of the divine justice and unicity". To emphasize the divine oneness, they rejected the distinction between divine attributes and divine essence and to emphasize divine justice, they taught that God is constrained to do what is good. They held that good and evil existed in objects and that reason can discern them.

The Mutazila have been called the "rationalists of Islam". In point of fact, their aim was to protect Muslim dogma from being misused by Greek philosophy, but in so doing they themselves made use of "philosophic" procedure. For some time they were in the ascendant at Baghdad and were the official exponents of Islam under the Abbasid caliph, Mamun. At this epoch the secular arm persecuted the "Ancients", who opposed the Mutazilite innovations and maintained that the Koranic text was uncreated. Blood was shed in this conflict. The great Ibn Hanbal was imprisoned and beaten with cudgels.

The Mutazila comprised two schools, one at Basra and one at Baghdad. At Basra, Abu 'l-Hudhayl al-Allaf al-Jubbai and his son Abu Hashim; at Baghdad, Bishr ben al-Mutamir and the two Jafar. The great commentator of the Koran, Zamakhshari, showed Mutazilite tendencies. His exegesis of many verses follows the metaphorical interpretation of the school.

3. In the fourth century A.H., Abu al-Hasan al-Ashari, who

gave up the Mutazilite school of thought, accused his erstwhile masters of betraying the pure transcendence of God and adopted Ibn Hanbal's views. He was the founder of the Asharite school, which for several hundred years was to be the principal trend of official Islamic thought. It was at its strongest under the caliph Mutawakkil and it persecuted the Mutazila. The greatest names in the science of *kalam* are to be found in the Asharite school: Baquillani, fourth to fifth centuries A.H. (tenth to eleventh A.D.), Juwayni, fifth century A.H. (eleventh A.D.), al-Ghazali, fifth to sixth century A.H. (eleventh to twelfth A.D.), Razi, sixth to seventh A.H. (twelfth to thirteenth A.D.), Iji, eighth century A.H. (fourteenth A.D.), Jurjani, eighth to ninth century A.H. (fourteenth to fifteenth A.D.), etc. The theories successively evolved and, still more, the methods of reasoning, sometimes differed considerably from those taught by Ashari himself. But however divergent the streams of Asharite thought, they have points in common: the Koran is uncreated, the mystery of God is beyond the reach of man, the divine attributes are real entities, the pre-excellence of the law over reason is absolute, secondary causes (in the philosophical meaning) are non-existent, there is no such thing as human freewill—man's acts are attributed to him and he is made juridically responsible for them, but God is the creator of good and evil and creator of human acts as of everything else. Good and evil have existence only in the commandments of God, who guides in goodness those whom he will and abandons those whom he wishes to abandon. Some Asharites, in an endeavour to safeguard divine transcendence, explain matter by a theory of discontinuity and atomism and a perpetual re-creation of things by God, the sole Agent (*agens*). The thought of this school came to a standstill in stereotyped manuals for students, such as those of Sanusi of Tlemcen (ninth century A.H.; fifteenth A.D.) and Bajuri (thirteenth A.H.: nineteenth A.D.).

4. Baghdad, the Abbasid capital, had witnessed the birth and triumph of the Asharite school. At the same epoch,

another school established itself farther to the East. This too was to be regarded as orthodox. It was named after al-Maturidi al-Samarkandi. The difference between the Asharite and Maturidite schools have been frequently studied. Briefly we may say that the fundamental problems of the Asharites receive at the hands of the Maturidites a more supple treatment, a more "psychological" approach. Thus, God created in man the "root" of his acts, but the human will "colours" them, gives them their moral "qualification". Noteworthy also are the differences in the teaching of the two schools on the divine attributes.

From another angle, the differences between the two schools may be traced in a considerable measure to their connections with different juridical schools. In this light it would be more correct to call the Maturidites Hanafite-Maturidites, while the Asharites are linked with the Shiites. As for the Mutalizites, when official Sunnite Islam rejected them, they became the inspiration of "schismatic" theology. Their influence was to be permanently felt by Kharijite and Shiite thought. The Hanbalite school alone, despite the reverence in which Ibn Hanbal was held by al-Ashari, persisted in denying the cogency of the science of *kalam*. The work by the Hanbalite mystic Ansari, entitled *Dham al-Kalam*, is one of the most virulent attacks ever made on the use of reason for the defence of dogma.

A subsidiary religious science: falsafa

The historical evolution of the schools of Kalam cannot be properly understood without reference to *falsafa*, that is, the Arab Muslim (sometimes Irano-Muslim) philosophy of Hellenistic inspiration. This is not a religious science. Its beginnings are in the infiltration of Greek thought in the ninth century A.D. (third century A.H.)—Plato, Aristotle, extracts from Plotinus and their commentators—translated into Arabic. Abu Yakub al-Kindi, the first of its great exponents, seems also to have been a doctor in *kalam*, or very nearly so: in a considerable number of his writings are to be found theories making for reconciliation between philosophy and the religious law. But very soon, in his successors, a severance between *falsafa* and *kalam* was effected. It is seen in Farabi (ninth to tenth century A.D., third to fourth A.H.), in Avicenna (tenth to eleventh century A.D., fourth to fifth centuries A.H.) and quite deliberately in Averroës (sixth century A.H.).

The individual fields of investigation of the "philosophers" (*falasifa*) correspond to various problems tackled by *kalam*. They themselves are all in favour of a conciliation between philosophy and law, but they dismiss the notion of subordination of philosophy to law put forward by Abu Yakub al-Kindi. The basis on which they sought to establish this conciliation was allegorical exegesis (*tawil*). It was in such exegesis that each of the great philosophers sought to discover in the Koran metaphorical expressions supporting his own tenets. Thus, a perhaps too literal continuity with Greek thought led the *falasifa* to affirm the temporal eternity of the created world, to think of creation as a willed but necessary emanation proceeding from the First Principle and to place the human act in the realm of universal determinism. The resurrection of the body does not fit into their conception of the world and the thesis of existence of one only *Intellectus agens*, propounded by Farabi and Averroës, throws doubt on the personal survival of the soul.

The chief antagonists of the earliest Asharites were the Mutazilites. The controversy was thus within the field of *kalam* itself. Very soon Asharites and Maturidites were to come face to face with the "philosophers". These found their most powerful adversaries in Ghazali and his contemporary, Shahrastani. So important was this controversy that it spread far beyond the boundaries of Islam. It pivoted mainly round a famous book. In the fifth to sixth centuries A.H., the great Ghazali figures as the outstanding reformer. Conceding that *kalam* might well serve as a "medicine" to cure the doubts of the hesitant, he himself claimed that there should be a reorientation of religious science, so that it centres on faith worked out in practical living. He set out to refute the errors—he would say, impieties—of the "philosophers", especially Farabi and Avicenna. Hence his great work, *The Incoherence of Philosophy* (*Tahafut al-Falasifa*). A century later in the Maghreb, at the extreme west of the Muslim world, Averroës produced an answer to it—incidentally his own apologia—entitled, *The Incoherence of the Incoherence* (*Tahafut al-tahafut*).

The influence of Averroës was especially felt in the Latin West, whereas Avicenna was to leave his mark unmistakably on Muslim thought. His commentator and champion was the Shiite, Nasir al-Din al-Tusi. Even at the present day, an Avicennian school may be said to exist in Iran. Even the Sunnites, who attacked his theory, came under his influence. Ghazali, earliest of all, in more than one instance borrowed materials from him. Several doctors of *kalam*, from the twelfth century onwards, followed suit. The historian Ibn Khaldun calls this trend the "modern school".

But in the long run this did not make for progress in either philosophical or theological thought. The treatises became encumbered beyond measure with rational "preambles" and dialectical discussions. Sometimes *kalam* and *falsafa* fused to produce only a hybrid theory to the detriment of both systems.

Looking back on the stagnation into which the age of commentators, glosses and manuals lulled both *kalam* and *falsafa*, one can readily understand the distrust with which their adversaries dismissed them, the Hanbalites for instance and the Zahiriya, who for a time deserved to be called ultra-Hanbalites. One outstanding adversary was Ibn Hazm of Cordova (tenth to eleventh century A.D.), who disassociated himself from all dialectics and speculation, in the name of the word of God and the evidence of language. All the same, in his demonstrations against his adversaries, Ibn Hazm, in self-defence, showed himself both philosopher and theologian: thus his analysis of the divine decree and the acts of man are instances of original thinking, undeniably superior to the corresponding studies done by the Asharites of the same period.

In any case, from the fifteenth century to the end of the nineteenth, *kalam*, as defensive apologetics, remained stagnant, chained to its set problems, churning over the self-same discussions and stereotyped refutations of *falsafa*. The only worthwhile attempt at a revival of thought is that made by Afghani and, more especially, Mohammed Abduh, at the end of the nineteenth and beginning of the twentieth centuries: both endeavoured to recast the defensive apologetics of Islam in the light of contemporary problems. But the paralysis contracted in previous centuries renders such efforts largely ineffective. In such fundamental questions as prophetism or freewill, the work done by Mohammed Abduh in his *Risalat al-tawid* are far from reaching the level of the analyses worked out by Ghazali or even such adversaries of *kalam* as Ibn Hazm or Ibn Taymiyya.

Must the science of *kalam* be satisfied with studying the history of its own past controversies, or is it capable of a revival? A revival would certainly call for a considerable recasting of its field of investigation and the adoption of an adequate philosophical framework. But that in turn postulates as a prerequisite the solution of the age-long antagonism between philosophy and law and of the further problem—which has never really been faced—of the relation between faith and reason. On these conditions, *kalam* might well develop beyond the limits of purely defensive apologetics and become real theology, that is, an effort of the intelligence to grasp faith. That would, indeed, be a novel undertaking in Islam. How it would all work out one cannot venture to suggest.

Ought Muslim mysticism to be classified as a branch of religious science? Ibn Khaldun includes it in his work and special courses in it are given in some of the great mosques. At the present day, as in the past, it has its adversaries, more numerous even than the opponents of *kalam*. Ever since the violent opposition it encountered in the first centuries, the official attitude of Islam has been ambiguous. But it would hardly do justice to Muslim mysticism were we to confine ourselves to its didactic content alone. In the next chapter we shall endeavour to assess it in regard to the problem of the human act (freewill) and the Last Ends.

There is a group of Arab sciences known as "instrumental sciences", which are looked on as associated with the religious sciences or as their ancillary sciences. Thus Arabic grammar and literature, history in so far as it is a record of the propagation of Islam, mathematics and astronomy in so far as they provide data for working out inheritance legislated for by *fiqh* or for fixing the dates and festivals of the lunar calendar. Medicine and agriculture are sometimes considered annex sciences, other branches of study, including *falsafa*, are dubbed "foreign sciences"; they are reckoned licit when they do not run counter to Koranic faith, but blameworthy, and even proscribed, when they do.

FAITH AND "NECESSARY" ARTICLES OF FAITH

Controversy has been rife in every branch of religious science. One school would condemn as tainted with "infidelity" (*kufr*) what another took to be the truth. But running through all these divisions of thought and sect, is there a lowest common denominator, as it were, of religious tenets accepted by all Muslims?

Ashari himself taught his disciples not to cast anathemas at anyone who happened to think otherwise than they. The traditional tag is well known: "He is a Muslim who prays turned towards Mecca." On this Ghazali laid stress in his autobiography. As we have seen, it can be said that for every Muslim, faith is witness. So fully is this held, that God is thought of as the supreme Believer, because he is the supreme Witness to himself and his revelation! Where the schools begin to go their own controversial way, is when they come to determine the content of witness and the manner in which it is to be borne. We may here set down some outstanding examples of this.

The act of faith

The earliest trends make the entirety of Koranic prescriptions the object of the act of faith, with regard to both truths to be believed and works to be done. So that faith would comprise interior acceptance plus witness by word plus good works. This definition, which was currently used by the Mutazilites, was also that of Ashari and, amongst others, Ghazali. The Kharijite schismatics had already promoted it. We shall see the bearing it had on the theories regarding the human act.

The Hanafite-Maturidite trend was to define faith as interior acceptance plus witness by word.

Taken as a whole, the Asharites departed from their founder's definition of faith. For them the formal element was *tasdek*, mental acceptance. Witness by word, they held, was a sign of faith and, except where circumstances made it impossible, it was obligatory, but it was not of the essence of faith. They taught that while faith was an interior and intangible thing, good works could increase its intensity, evil works diminish it.

In connection with this another problem arises regarding the relationship between faith (*iman*) and *islam* taken to mean the observances of an organized religion. The definitions of these terms vary from school to school, some identify them, some distinguish between them. The normal state of the believer is to be a believer *and* a Muslim. But it is possible to make an exterior profession of *islam* without an interior conviction; similarly, one could be a believer interiorly, and thus be in order in the sight of God, while never having the opportunity of making an exterior profession of *islam*.

One and all, the schools condemn—as does the Koran—the "hypocrites" (*munafikun*), who put on a façade of adherence to Islam without being sincere believers and bring trouble and rebellion into the Community. Witness by word makes a man a Muslim in the eyes of men, but this has no worth in the sight of God unless it is matched by intimate conviction.

The content of faith

The dogmatic content of witness to faith is summed up in the two parts of the *Shahada*: the oneness of God and the mission of Mohammed, his envoy. "There is no God but God and Mohammed is his prophet."

At an early date, the schools elaborated, from the Koranic text and the *hadith*, a body of propositions which were considered essential and had to be known and professed explicitly. A famous passage of the Koran (2, 285) states: "Believers believe in God, his angels, his books, his envoys." And this finds an echo in a no less famous *hadith*: "Faith is to believe in God, his angels and the prophets and resurrection." Another, often quoted, says: "And to believe in the divine decree regarding good and evil, the sweet and the bitter." Lastly, we may quote: "The Prophet has said: Man has not the faith unless he believes in four things, that he bear witness that there is no divinity save God (no God but God); that I am the Envoy God sent to teach the truth; that he believe in the resurrection of the dead; that he believe in the divine decree regarding good and evil, the sweet and the bitter."

Taking these texts together, we find:

1. Absolute oneness of God, merciful and omnipotent creator, unfathomable in the mystery of his nature and power, yet "very close" to the man who prays, and the Judge of Judges.

2. God one and transcendent has spoken to mankind and imposed his law on them through his prophets and envoys. The three great legislator-prophets are Moses, who at God's bidding promulgated the Torah, Jesus, who promulgated the Gospel, Mohammed, who promulgated the Koran, which sums up and sets the seal on all prophecy. Many are the other prophets and envoys who must be believed. The Koran and the traditions record the history of the principal ones amongst them, from Adam to St John the Baptist. The Muslim faith is rooted in the faith of Abraham, indeed claims to *be* the faith of Abraham, the "friend of God".

3. The existence of the angels who, says a tradition, were created from light. It was, they say, through the angel Gabriel that the Koran was brought to Mohammed. The angels are the bearers of God's commands and they intervene with men. When the angels were put to the test, Iblis (Satan) revolted. There are also intermediary beings called *jinn*, created from fire, subjects of the law, some of them good, some tempters.

4. At the last hour—which is always imminent—every being that is a subject of the law will, at God's command, rise again to be judged and thereafter enjoy eternal delights or eternal torments in hell. God is "the King of the Day of Judgement".

The professions of faith insist on the reality of the material details of the Last Day: the Bridge and Gehenna, the Scales of Judgement, the list on which man's acts are recorded, the Basin of the Prophet from which the elect drink, the Pen, the Guarded Table, the Throne of God. The main trends of thought, Asharite and Hanafite-Maturidite, teach that these objects of another world really exist but without explaining how (*bila kayf*), that is, without it being possible to derive an accurate notion of them from similar objects in this world.

5. The predetermining decree of God in regard to good and evil. The Koran teaches both the absolute omnipotence of God and human responsibility, but does not formulate the ensuing problem of predestination. Positive predestination to evil is a doctrine held by only one school (the Asharites) and

is not directly taught by the Koran itself. Belief in the "divine decree" (*kadar*) demands, above all, remitting of self to God's power, in an act of abandonment (*tawakkul*) which is unquestioning, and is one lasting continuous and single witness to inaccessible Transcendency.

There are many other angles from which Muslim dogmas may be viewed. A great deal has been written on the subject. But the points we have made seem representative of the essential content of the act of faith and the resultant interior attitude of the believer. Such are the "necessary" articles of faith, without which one cannot be a Muslim. They are the basis which each school or "creed" studies and elaborates in its own way. Throughout all the complexity and wealth of Islamic religious sciences, sincere and explicit adherence to the five points listed above are, as it were, the dogmatic texture of the entire Community of Believers.

APPENDIX TO CHAPTER IV

THE SECTS

As we have seen in Chapter II, after the Battle of Siffin (37 A.H.), the Muslim Community split up into three groups: 1. The Sunnis, faithful to the customs of the Prophet (*sunnat al-nabi*). They were in the majority and even today count ninety per cent. of Islam. Most of the analyses and descriptions given in this present work refer to them. 2. Kharijites, "seceders". 3. Shiites, from *shia*, the "party" (of Ali). We cannot follow in detail their extremely complex history, but shall set down briefly their main trends and approaches to religious questions.

Kharijites

The origin of the schisms in Islam lay in the differences over the caliphate or supreme imamate and the conditions for its legitimacy. It will be remembered that the Sunnis held that the caliph must be of the Quraysh tribe, though many doctors were later prepared to accept as legitimate caliph, if necessity so urged, a member of another tribe or even a non-Arab. In principle the caliph must be designated by the people who "bind and unbind", and must receive their allegiance; contemporary reformers stress the elective character of the office. But it was admitted that the caliph could designate his successor, for in doing this he was considered to be acting as the representative of the notables. Lastly, by the "law of necessity", power could be seized by military force. The essential point in all this is that the caliph, before his accession to the throne, must enjoy the physical qualities required in a caliph and be endowed with the "status of justice" (*adala*). But once he has been elected or designated, he is once and for all the *locum tenens* of the Prophet, whatever he may do in his private life, so long as he continues to promote publicly the "rights of God and of man" and does not order anything contrary to the Koranic law.

By contrast, the Kharijites soon came to demand of the caliph a blameless life both in his official and private capacity, so that a caliph or imam who committed a "grave fault" or left the "straight path" could cease to be legitimate. The Kharijites had been partisans of Ali but they disapproved of his conduct at the battle of Siffin and his acceptance of arbitration at the dictates of Muawiya. So they took up the idea that requirements of race and tribe should not be considered in the choice of the imam. Any sincere believer, even a "negro slave", can be elected, they say, if he is a model Muslim. Further, the Community has a strict obligation to place itself under the authority of an Imam.

As a consequence of these views, the Kharijites hold that works come necessarily into the definition of faith. A Muslim who commits a "grave fault" is an apostate. Carried to its full limits, this implies that all non-Kharijites are in fact apostates. Some of their doctors make no distinction between Muslims and Christians or Jews who say: "Mohammed is God's envoy to the Arabs, not to us."

The Kharijites were often characterized by frantic fanaticism. They were drawn mostly from the mass of the people and their inflexibility did not even baulk at "religious murder". This gave rise to innumerable insurrections and wars. Their egalitarian principles were held in honour by the *Mawali*, who would always meet with disdain from the Arabs of the Umayyad Empire.

Amongst the Kharijites the following views are found.

(a) Extremists. 1. The Azraqites hold that whoever departs from the straight path by a grave fault can never again return to the faith and, together with his kin, must be condemned to death. They were ardent supporters of the principle of "religious murder". They set themselves up as a State in southern Iran and were eventually exterminated in a terrible war at the end of the seventh century A.H.

2. The Yazidiyya (founded by Yazid b. Unaysa) do not hold that the Koran is the final seal of prophecy. They teach that a prophet will come amongst the Iranians and will institute a fourth religion, a celestial religion, none other than the Sabeans, of whom the Koran speaks. This group must not be confused with the Yazidis, or Yezidis.

(b) Moderate tendencies. 1. The Sufrites, who allow temporary abstention from war against non-Kharijites and permit *takiyya*, that is, dissimulation of faith (of which, below). They were later absorbed into the Ibadite group, which was founded by Abd Allah b. Ibad and is of far greater importance.

2. The Ibadites are first found in 129 A.H. (A.D. 747). They are the only Kharijites extant today and are in Oman and at Zanzibar. In the second century A.H. they were the motive power behind the great Berber movement in the West, and came very near to dominating the whole of North Africa. Defeated by the Abbasids in 772, they reorganized themselves as the Rustamid principality of Tahert, which was ultimately destroyed by the Shiite-Fatimid onslaught in 296 A.H. (A.D. 908–9). Notable Ibadite groups, usually called Abadites, still

exist at the present day at Wargla, Djebel Nefusa, the Isle of Djerba and, more particularly, in the Mzab, where they have set themselves up as an egalitarian community and religious unit (Mzabites). Ibadism has been crossed and re-crossed by politico-religious dissensions.

It would not be possible here to give a full exposition of Ibadite doctrine. We may note that they set aside *ijma* and *qiyas* and make use of *ray* (the opinion of the prudent man) instead. On many points their doctrines were influenced by the Mutazilite doctors. Small offences were pardoned by God; serious faults could only be effaced by repentance. The Koran, which is the word of God, is created; there is no vision of God in after-life.

Since the destruction of the principality of Tahert, the Ibadites have thought of themselves as being in a "state of obscurity". Hence, certain laws of the Community, such as the obligatory office of Imam, remain in abeyance until the day when their "state of glory" will be restored.

Shia

In the history of Islamic political and religious thought, Shia plays a far more important role than the Kharijites. There have been times when it dominated vast areas of the Muslim world; many of its thinkers, even those of extreme views, proved to be a precious leaven in the elaboration of the religious sciences. Later, it was to become firmly established among the Iranians, but we must not overlook the fact that it is of Arab origin.

In the crucial question of the true position of the imamate (caliphate), the Shiites were to be the "legitimists", resolutely loyal to the "people of the House" and the descendants of Ali. Devotion to the family of the Prophet is a common bond among them. They do not accept as legitimate the first three caliphs, Abu Bakr, Umar, Uthman, and consequently they reject the *ijma* of the Companions and, for still more obvious reasons, the consensus of the Community as such. They do not recognize any Sunna whose authenticity cannot be traced back to the "people of the House". Their collections of traditions, called *akhbar* instead of *hadith*, coincide with the Sunnite traditions, but have their own distinctive chains of transmitters.

The Shiite notion of Community is built round the rôle of the imam as descendant of Ali. The imam is not only infallible but also impeccable, guaranteed, like the prophets, against all fault. But disagreement over the list of legitimate imams of the past proved to be one of the main grounds of division within Shia itself. The predominant opinion, called imamite, holds that there have been twelve imams. The last of them, however, is thought of as still living, mysteriously hidden, or absent (*ghaib*), awaiting the hour of his manifestation.

Having rejected *ijma*, the Shiites make a great deal of *ijtihad* (individual research made by the doctors, who are the mouthpiece of the hidden imam). Hence these doctors, residing for the most part in the "holy cities" of Shia, are the spiritual power. With the "disappearance" of the last of the legitimate imams, the chief executive power can now be vested only in a temporal sovereign. The existence of a fully organized system of temporal power in the earthly commonwealth is thus made possible.

The religious susceptibilities and the piety of the Shiites have characteristics all their own. One striking feature is the cult of hyperdulia paid to Ali and his close relatives, especially his wife Fatima and his sons Husan and Husayn. These were the four, it will be remembered, who were with Mohammed on the occasion of the *Mubahala* at Medina. The "passion" of Ali and Husayn—their "martyrdom"—came to be celebrated by a great number of commemorations, such as the famous procession of penitents and flagellants. Connected with this, came a sense of the redemptive worth of suffering and even the notion of redemption itself—a notion unknown to the Sunnis. The "holy cities" held, to say the least, in the same esteem as Mecca and Medina, are Kerbela (Iraq), the scene of the "passion" of Husayn, and Mashed (Iran), where the tombs of the "martyrs" are. The extremists carry their cult beyond hyperdulia and actually deify the race of Ali. There is also among the Imamites an ever active cult of the invisible and hidden imam: a devotional aspect of their expectation of the last hour.

A belief held throughout Islam is that the Mahdi will come at the end of time to lead all believers in the straight path, and will establish a reign of justice and make ready for the day of judgement. The Mahdi is variously identified with Mohammed, Christ or al-Khidr, the mysterious companion of Moses. Shiite piety and doctrine adopted the idea of the Mahdi as Master of the Last Day, and held that he would be Ali himself or one of his descendants. Christ would be his assistant. Shiite Mahdis have often in the course of history given rise to popular movements and sometimes have even had their share in the beginnings of the great empires.

There is a wealth of Shiite theology but it has still only been partially studied. Its impact on Muslim thought has been considerable. Like its opponents, the Kharijites, it uses materials derived from Mutazilism. But at an early date it borrowed from the traditional philosophy of ancient Persia or the Pythagorean and neo-Platonic thought of Greece. The double scheme of emanation and light (and therefore illumination) is at the heart of its concept of the world. It has its own answers to the problems of faith and salvation. In the practical field and in places where Shia was in the minority, we may note the use made of *takiyya* (*kitman*), concealment of faith as regards verbal witness and acts of worship, provided faithful witness (right intention) is borne in one's heart. There are also some variations in the application of canon law. To give one example, with the exception of the Zaidites, Shia permits temporary marriages, the duration of which is agreed on when the parties enter upon the marriage bond. This form of marriage was elaborated for a time by Mohammed and was abolished by Umar I. Since Shia does not recognize Umar's claim to the imamate, they ignore his ruling.

The Shiites had broken off from the main Muslim body on rather flimsy claims, and, as often happens in such cases, they themselves subsequently split up into numerous sects. Chief among these are:

1. The Zaidis. These are the most moderate of the Shiites, close in belief and sentiment to the Sunnis. They limit the legitimate imams to five, and, contrary to other movements, acknowledge Zaid b. Ali, grandson of Husayn, as an imam. As many as eight variant tendencies are said to exist amongst the Zaidis. Their criterion for the legitimacy of an imam bears a strong resemblance to those of the Sunnis, but with this distinctly Shiite characteristic that he must be an Alid. They agree, however, that the Medinan Community did not default in choosing Abu Bakr and Umar, but assert that Ali would have been a better choice because of his personal qualifications.

Hence, they do not believe in a hidden and invisible imam. They hold that from the time of Zaid's death, the imamate should be elective. The elected sovereign enjoys divine assistance to keep him in the ways of righteousness, but he is essentially no different from other men. The *dai*, or preachers, hold a key position in the Zaidi groups. Lastly, we may note their rejection of temporary marriages. The Zaidis were predominant on the shores of the Caspian Sea until A.D. 1126 (520 A.H.). There they brought into existence the sect of Nuktawis. Towards 860 A.H., they founded the State of Yemen which, of course, remains in existence today. Its entry into the United Arab States may well create a new interest in Zaidism. But Zaidis and Sunnis have so much in common that some orthodox reformers conceived the idea of making the Imam of Yemen the supreme caliph of the Muslim Community.

2. The largest body of Shia are the Imamites or Twelvers, so called because they acknowledge a succession of twelve legitimate imams and believe in the cult of the hidden imam.

They hold that a particle of divine light resides by emanation in the imam and guarantees his impeccability. The general characteristics of Shia, which we have described above, refer especially to the Twelvers. As many as eleven variant parties exist amongst them, corresponding to their divergent views on the Alid succession. From the time of the Safawids, Imamism has been the official religion of Persia.

3. Extremist Imamites can be grouped under the Ismailiya, or Seveners. These limit the number of legitimate imams to seven. The last of them was Ismail b. Jafar, who will come again at the end of time as the Mahdi. The Ismailiya are extremists in the sense that they came to divinizing the Alid race, thus, in the eyes of all other Mohammedans, imperilling the doctrine of the absolute oneness of God and detracting from the prerogative of the Prophet in favour of the "People of the House". Their opponents, Imamites and Sunnis, castigate them with the term *ghulat* ("one who goes beyond all bounds" in the matter of belief). It is indeed amongst the Ismailiya that one encounters the greatest number of Shiite thinkers and writers who, even indirectly through what their adversaries wrote of them, influenced the religious and cultural outlook of Islam. Thus for instance Nasir Khosraw and the Ismailian trends of the great encyclopaedia of the *Ikhwan al-Safa* (Brethren of the Purity, or Sincere Brethren). Avicenna tells us that his father and eldest brother were converted to Ismailiya, and Ghazali, who had undertaken to refute Ismailiya, found himself attacked for having substantiated their doctrine. Moreover, the Carmathian politico-religious movement, which was of such great importance, was also Ismailian; so were the founders of the great Fatimid Empire.

Their concept of the world is essentially emanantist. Between God and matter lies a chain of seven principles, corresponding to the seven cycles of imams. The Mutazilite *tatil*, which "purified" the notion of divine attributes so thoroughly that it ended in rejecting it altogether, has its place in the

Ismailian "unmanifested God". Thence, by his commandment, emanates the Universal Intellect, "God manifested", to whom the prayers of the faithful are addressed. From the Intellect emanates the universal soul (or reason) and thence proceeds the pure passivity of primary matter. The soul tends to return to the Intellect in quest of its own perfection and it is this urge to reascend that explains the coming of man. Time and space exist as first principles.

There was a system of initiation by seven or nine degrees, linked with a secret and highly allegorical meaning of the Koran. In the matter of Koranic exegesis the Ismailiya are *batiniyya* (*batin*: that which is interior, intimate, hidden).

Parallels could be established here with, for instance, the emanantism of Avicenna, and many of the Ismailian lines of thought were to influence the later Sufis of the "Unicity of Being". A mystical hierarchy, moreover, extended from the *natik* (prophetic voice) incarnate in the Prophet, the *asas*, his interpreter (Ali), the imam, the *hujja* (proof), right down to the *dai* (missionary preachers). The political rôle of the Ismailian *dai* was sometimes considerable.

Various Ismailian sects

There are the Carmathians, with their broad, popular movement of theocratic communism, the neo-Ismailian Fatimids with their brilliant empire, the Khuja, the Indian sect of the Aga Khan, the Hashishin (Assassins) with their principle of blind obedience. The Druzes (there are some 150,000 of them in Syria and the Lebanon) hold a kind of Ismailian heresy. In 1017, the Fatimid Caliph Hakim "revealed" that he was the divinity itself. The sect was founded by Hamza, who was looked on as the incarnation of the Universal Intellect. Then came the incarnation of the Universal Soul, of the word, of the right or preceding wing, of the left or following wing. The name Druze comes from Darazi, a missionary (*dai*), who recognized and preached the "revelation" of Hakim and even sought to supplant Hamza. The Nusairi professed belief in the divinity of Ali with Salmon as his precursor and Mohammed as his emanation. The most important Nusairi group are the Alawis. The same trends are found in a more recent sect, the Ali-Ilahi. The Metwali are a further Ismailian derivation.

We cannot here follow the Ismailiya throughout their history. At the present time they are to be found in groups of varying tendencies in Syria, the Lebanon, in certain regions of Iran, Central Asia, Afghanistan and Kafiristan. They are numerous in Oman. In India and Pakistan and the African coast of Zanzibar, they number some 300,000, amongst whom the supporters of the Aga Khan are recruited.

Other Sects

The Yezidis: These consist of the Kurd tribes who today do not number more than 70,000. They are found in Iraq, Syria, Armenia and Iran. The basis of their belief seems to be derived from ancient Manichean traditions combined with Assyrian, Christian (Nestorian and Jacobite) and especially Muslim influences. It has been wrongly suggested that they are connected with Yazi b. Unaysa. It is sometimes said also that their name comes from Yazid b. Muawiya, by whom they claim they were restored, not founded. They profess that the only son of Adam was their founder. A further etymology is suggested by the modern Persian word *ized* (angel, deity).

Their spoken language and "liturgical" language is Kurdish, though their two sacred books, written they say before creation, are in Arabic. In their beliefs they distinguish between God the creator—who having created remains passive—and Malak-Taus, the Essence of God manifested in execution of the divine will, who is one with God, God's *alter ego*. Divine or semi-divine beings act as intermediaries between God and man.

The Yezidis believe in metempsychosis, reject the eternity of hell and the reality of evil. They are often referred to as the "adorers of the devil" (Shayton is the name of Malak-

Taus), but that is not true. They themselves take the name of adorers of God (*esidi*). The notion of the devil, "father of evil", has no place in their doctrine.

They have strikingly peculiar family, social and "liturgical" customs. Their civic organization is theocratic and esoteric. A distinction is made between the *murid* (novices) or laity and the *ruhan*, *kahan* or clerics. The latter are subdivided into six classes. Nobody during their lifetime may pass from one class to another; they are almost separate castes. At the summit is the supreme Shaykh and the Emir.

The Yezidis show great reverence for many of the Muslim Sufi saints, especially Shaykh Adi, Hasan Basri and Abd al-Qadir Jilani.

The sect seems to have come into being in Syria under the Umayyads. Since they had neither Koran nor Torah nor Gospel, they met with severe condemnation from the doctors of Islam and were more than once persecuted.

The nineteenth century saw the rise of three new syncretist Muslim sects. In India, Ghulam Ahmad (1839–1908) founded the Ahmadiyya. He claimed to have received a direct revelation from God and to work miracles. The Ahmadiyya acknowledge that Mohammed is the final seal of the prophecy but affirm that Ghulam Ahmad is also a prophet. They allow themselves to come under Hindu influence and profess a cult for Christ who, they say, was not crucified but went to die on Indian soil at Srinagar. In their teaching and their way of life there is a form of late Muslim Sufism, such as exists in India, activated by modern Western infiltrations. A minority group, Ahmadiyya Anjuman, reject Ghulam Ahmad as a prophet and recognize him only as *mujtihad* (one who practises *ijtihad*, which was explained above). It is in this latter form that the Ahmadiyya are best known outside their own country. They have established numerous missions and made conversions in many countries: Indonesia, the U.S.A., Berlin and in London, where they have built mosques and publish reviews. Islam as represented by them is strongly tainted with modern intellectual liberalism. Official Islam has declared them heretical.

In Iran, Babism, of Muslim Shiite origin, made its appearance as a new religion. In 1844, Mizra Ali Muhammad declared himself the Bab, that is, the gateway . . . to knowledge of divine truth. He rallied the *mahdist* ("messiah") expectations. He even put himself forward as a new revealed Koran. For legal purity he substituted a purity based on temperance. Important social reforms were stipulated: abolition of repudiation, emancipation of women. Gnostic interpretations of Ismailian origin stress the mystical value of numbers.

Faced with the magnitude and success with which this movement was propagated, the Iranian Government intervened. After stubborn resistance in armed conflict, the Babis were defeated and Mirza Ali was shot. In the midst of a bloody skirmish, a woman, Qurrat al-Ayn ("easy-on-the-eye"), a remarkable propagandist and initiator of feminine emancipation in Iran, was strangled and burnt at the stake.

The influence of Babism disappeared little by little. In 1863 a new sect, an off-shoot of Babism, known as the Bahahi, began to spread. It was founded by Baha Allah ("splendour of God"). There is hardly a trace of Islam in it. It proclaims itself as having been foretold by the Bab and sent to found a universal religion, which unites and sums up all existing religions. It has no rites, no hierarchy, it stands for universal friendship and equality and the reconciliation of all men and things in the love of God alone. Subsequently, it drew more and more on modern Western and humanitarian ideas.

CHAPTER V

MAN'S ACTS AND HIS DESTINY

MORAL VALUES: THE "COMMANDERY" OF RECTITUDE

When the Koran, in the Medinan *Suras*, sets out to sketch the Muslim Community in a few bold lines, it simultaneously emphasizes witness to faith in God and a moral code for man's acts. "Ye are the best people that hath been raised up into mankind. Ye enjoin the just and forbid evil" (*Sura* 3, 110).

What does this "commandery" of rectitude imply? Ibn Taymiyya explains: "To order that which is good (proper) means to see that Muslims say the prescribed prayers, give the legal alms, keep the fast and make the pilgrimage; to see that they are sincere and loyal and grateful to their parents and that they keep on good terms with their neighbours."[1] This enumeration is, however, by no means exhaustive. There are other duties imposed by the Koran: hospitality, protection of the feeble and the orphan, shunning debauchery and, to sum up, fidelity to the given word. "Oh believers! be faithful to your engagements" (*Sura* 5, 1). Engagements towards God and engagements towards man—each inseparable from the other—fidelity to the pact whereby the Muslim Community is constituted, that is to be the perfection of righteousness. The "commandery of rectitude", understood in this way, gives the office of supreme imam or caliph its true meaning—

[1] *Siyasa shariyya,* Henri Laoust (Damascus–Beirut, 1948).

he is the preceptor and leader of the Community. But every Muslim must contribute to the best of his ability to the furtherance of these aims.

THE SALVATION OF MAN

Sin and repentance

However much their views on the nature of the Koran may differ,[2] all Muslim schools of thought are at one in acknowledging its text as the criterion of morality. Thus, the good consists in obeying God by conformity with his commandments; evil consists in disobeying him.[3] The evil act, prevarication—*khata, dhanab*—is essentially disobedience, *masiyya.*

A useful comparison may be drawn between *masiyya* and the Christian notion of sin. Islam looks on sin or prevarication as first and foremost disobedience to the (positive) Law of God. God cannot be affected by sin—he is immutable and inaccessible. This is frequently illustrated by a comparison with the sultan and his slave. No act of the slave can affect the personality of the sultan, and if the slave is disobedient, the sultan may, just as he pleases, use clemency and pardon him or use justice and punish him.

This extrinsic notion of the relationship between God and man is very much in keeping with the notion of divine "voluntarism" professed by the Asharite school. But it by no means accounts for the full content of the basic Muslim notion. Disobedience towards God cannot affect him; but it does violate the "rights of God and of man", which the Community, by God's command, must promote on this earth. It thus entails a violation of the pact which God granted to Adam's race, a pact which makes the slave a believer and entitles him to enter into relationship with God. And in

[2] Cf. Chapter 4, above.

[3] Thus the terms *huquq* and *hudud* (penal rights and limits) are complementary.

numerous passages in the Koran God has affirmed his benevolence towards the servant who obeys him. For example, in *Sura* 2, 192: "God loveth those who do good." What is more, he promises *ridwan*, God's good pleasure, towards those who submit to him. This will be the great bliss (*Sura* 9, 73). The "soul at rest returns to the Lord, satisfied and pleasing to him" (*Sura* 89, 27–8). This implies a kind of mutual bond between God and the faithful believer. There is here no question of sanctifying grace in the Christian sense of divine indwelling.[4] God's good pleasure, gracious satisfaction, is represented as a status (*hukm*) in which God places his servant if he deigns to guide him in the "straight way". The opposite of this is abandonment by God (*khidhlan*) not a mere negation but something positive—which *results* in disobedience.

In the field of imputability, Muslim tradition has always recognized two kinds of faults—"small" and "great". These notions do not tally with the definition of mortal and venial sin in Catholic theology. Or rather, for Islam, the only mortal sin in the strict meaning of the word is apostasy. If denial of faith is only interior, the impious remains "a believer in the sight of men"; but only God shall judge of this, he who alone knows the heart of man and abhors hypocrisy (*Sura* 63). In the case of external apostasy, the Community shall visit chastisement on the sinner pending the chastisement of God.

But the distinction between "great" and "small" faults is not determined on the basis of *aversio a Deo* and *conversio ad creaturam*. "Great faults" are not faults which entail the loss of participation in the divine life, the life of grace. They are simply disobedience to prescriptions laid down by God as essential.

There is no clearly defined list of these and they vary from author to author. We may note, however, that failure to

[4] Though one might possibly find something suggestive of it. We shall see this more fully below, in dealing with some of the mystics.

observe obligatory acts of worship does not of itself constitute a grave fault. For a grave fault there must be deliberate contempt for the commandments of God or rejection of faith.

A widely read text-book gives the following list of grave faults. Apostasy and denial of faith, accusing the Prophet of falsehood or despising him, murder of a human being whom God forbids to kill, fornication and adultery, sins against nature, ill-treatment of father or mother, black magic, serious calumny, flight in the day of assault, usury, and "other similar faults". Many authors add to these the use of fermented beverages and serious theft. These faults are, so to speak, the counterpart of the positive acts prescribed by the "commandery of rectitude".

These various faults incur *hudud*, the penalties prescribed by the Koran. If they violate both the "rights of God and the rights of man", the penalties imposed are severe corporal punishments and of a public nature; if only the "rights of man" are violated, punishment of a private nature may be deemed sufficient.

But the fault, whether public or private, punished by human justice or unknown, remains an act of personal disobedience to divine positive law as long as the culprit has not duly repented and amended his heart. The Muslim doctors make it quite clear: no grave fault can be "effaced" unless it is followed by repentance (*tawba*). Now there are three essential conditions for valid repentance:

1. Relinquishing the conditions associated with the sin;
2. Being sorry for it in regard to God alone ("for the face of God", *li waj Allah*) and not for a mere motive of personal fear;
3. Having a firm determination not to commit it again.[5]

In regard to God there is no question of reparation, for sin

[5] Cf. Bajuri, *Hashiya . . . ala Jawharat al-tawhid* (Cairo, 1934), pp. 115–554. There is clearly a relation between *tawba* and Christian contrition.

cannot attain him. But if the "disobedience" towards God entails an injustice towards men, reparation for that is obligatory. If the culprit is absolutely unable to do so, the validity of his repentance will depend on his sincerity. It is for him to send up to God abundant prayers, that, in the day of judgement, those whom he has offended may forgive him his debt.

Muslim morality, unlike Christian morality, does not turn round the theological virtue of charity and interior penance. Nevertheless, God does enter into its formal motive. What makes a thing morally good or bad is determined by the Muslim in terms of obedience to the divine law. Repentance, we have seen, is only valid if it is "in the face of God". This is borne out by the list of "grave faults". True enough, with the exception of the Mutazilite school, the criterion of morality is first and foremost a positive law in the hands of the inscrutable divine will. But for all that, its content tallies very largely with the natural moral law, which is a reflection of divine wisdom written in creation and in the heart of man.[6] It has not been thought of in that way by Muslim schools in the past but there is nothing in the Koran to contradict the idea. Fragments of the Ten Commandments are found scattered here and there in Koranic law.

Judgement and future life

These demands are made in their totality at the level of the Community conceived as the "land of justice" (*dar al-adl*). Can it be said that they are less rigorous when it is a question of the destiny of each individual and the salvation of each believer severally? The answer is not that moral values are in this case lessened but that the effect on them of the "extrinsic" relationship of man to God here comes into play. The Muslim notion of repentance, we have seen,

[6] Not of course in their acceptance of polygamy. We shall see below that polygamy, though legislated for in the Koran, is not imposed by it.

closely resembles the Christian notion of contrition. But the measure in which that repentance is necessary for salvation is, as it were, relative. It is only absolutely necessary in the case of "grave faults against faith".

The Koran, especially in the Medinan *Suras*, emphasized the terrors of the judgement, the last hour when "heaven would gape wide open" (69, 16). Hell and heaven are eternal. The texts describe the happiness of the elect "on the right hand" and the torments of the damned. The paradise of the elect is spoken of as an amassing of the good things of creation but, despite the literal trends once current, these have nothing in common with the pleasures of this world. The crowning happiness of all, the supreme favour, will be the direct vision of God.[7] This is an intermittent and non-transforming vision. However, thanks to Greek and Christian influences, there has long since been a tendency, especially among mystics, to represent it as a vision that can never be lost.

It is only the Kharijites and the Mutazilite schools who teach that a grave fault that has not been effaced means the loss of this paradise and eternal hell. They alone hold that for the sinful believer who has not validly repented there is no possible intercession on the day of judgement. The existence of an intercession of that kind was asserted at an early date on the basis of a text (*Sura* 21, 28), which at first sight seems to refer to the angels. It is thus claimed that Mohammed will intercede for his Community and each prophet-envoy for his own people. This is *intercession* and not *mediation* and depends entirely on the benevolence of God, but the *hadith* insistently picture the "bronze portals of intercession" opening at the prayer of the Prophet of Islam.

Thus, in current teaching, as we have already said, the only sin that is irremediable and will be irremediably

[7] Koran, 75, 22–3 and 10, 26. The Mutazilites, however, give these passages a different interpretation, for they deny that it is possible to "see God".

punished in everlasting hell is an obstinate denial of faith in the One God and in the mission of his Envoy. Certainly, every sin of which the culprit validly repents is thereby "effaced" and there is in Islam no real equivalent of purgatory. But if there is no repentance and if faith in God remains, the punishment, by reason of that faith, cannot be eternal. In the end, the sinner who remains a believer will come to the joys of paradise. He should indeed fear the terrible punishments that have been decreed. He will first be chastised in his tomb, and then, after the resurrection, in hell. But his stay in hell will be only transitory. Furthermore, if there is no repentance, God can still show himself, according to his Word, the Indulgent, the Ready Pardoner. The sincere believer who has committed grave faults and has not repented or does not repent in the face of God alone, knows that he can, through the intercession of the Prophet, throw himself on the mercy of God. God, should he so wish, will give him entry into paradise without delay.[8] "Perchance the Lord will efface your wicked deeds" (66, 8).

Mention must here be made of an intermediary place, the *araf* (7, 46–9), a notion that is greatly debated. Some say it is something like limbo, some kind of "neutral" situation for non-Muslim children and where also adult men whose evil deeds balance out their good actions stay for a time. The primary notion is that of a place of waiting. Some introduce the added notion of purification—an approximation to the notion of purgatory, perhaps borrowed from it.

But strictly speaking, Islam holds that faith alone saves, a jealous and exclusive faith, which is the only gift worthy to be offered to God. "If you join partners to God, vain shall be all your work" (Koran 39, 65). Compared with this total gift offered as witness to divine Transcendence, "good" or "evil" acts, commanded or forbidden, are dwarfed and assume a very relative value, enveloped as they are in the

[8] This is the Asharite teaching. Maturidites hold that there will be sinner-believers who will undergo temporary punishment.

benevolent pity of the Most High towards this frail being "composed of blood and slime", whom he deigns, notwithstanding, to call to proclaim him his Lord.[9]

God, says the Koran, is at the same time inaccessible and very close to man, his creature (Koran 6, 103). But this proximity itself in no way lessens the absolute inaccessibility. Grave faults which are not against faith are severely condemned when considered at the social level of the Community, but, considered in regard to the salvation of the individual, they are left to the decree of God's good pleasure. Ultimately, the only thing that counts is predetermination to faith, the supreme mercy. Salvation is not a participation in divine life: it is witness given to the One God and his Utterance, to which the believer makes a total abandonment of himself.

MUSLIM MYSTICISM

Men thirsting for God

From the earliest days of Islam there were men given to God who could not find full satisfaction in this extrinsic relationship to God and this falling back on faith alone, however rigorous and complete that faith might be. If God, through his prophets, has communicated his Word to men, how could a sincere heart not thirst to live by it in the very depths of his being and come thus one day to an encounter with the Interlocutor? Even in Mohammed's day, the sceptical Meccans jeered at him as the "man in love with his God". There was always in Islam an uninterrupted line of men thirsting for God, who endeavoured to encounter him by an inward living of the mystery. That, we believe, fundamentally accounts for the "people of *tasawwuf*", or Sufis, the mystics of Islam.

The earliest circles of Sufis first set out to devise a rule of life nurtured by inward meditation on the Koran. Wearing

[9] In the context, of course, of the "pact" of pre-eternity. Cf. Koran, 7, 172.

patched tunics or woollen robes (*suf*), it was not long before the earliest ascetics began to group together. This was not really a monastic life but a group consisting of a master, *shaykh*, and his disciples.

But in the third century A.H., there was a rupture between the Sufis and the Islamic doctors and jurists. The condemnation and execution of Hallaj in A.D. 922 (309 A.H.) made the rupture irreparable. It was not until Ghazali (Algazel, A.D. 1059–1111) studied the matter that the underlying notions of the Sufis were directly taken up again and integrated into the official teaching. Yet right up to the present day, it has been asserted over and over again, even by those whose studies lie closest to the Koran and tradition, that there is no such thing as real mysticism in Islam.[10]

Opposition to the notion is explained as follows. At an early date, the term and notion of the love of God and of the mutual love of God and man gained currency in Sufism. This was no departure from the Koran. On the contrary, it sprang from meditating and acting on two famous verses, the only ones where this mutual love is dealt with: "Say: If ye love God, then follow me; God will love you and forgive you your sins" (3, 31). And: "O ye who believe! should any of you desert his religion, God will raise up other men loved by him and loving him" (5, 54). Sufism in the first centuries—and at that epoch the Sufi milieu and the traditionist milieu often criss-crossed—is seen as one of the spiritual virtualities offered to Muslims. Rabia, the convert flute player (eighth century A.D.) offered to God as a gift worthy of him, not only faith in the One God, but a faith animated by total and disinterested love: "And as to the love which seeks to render to Thee that of which Thou art worthy; Ah! to see no more the creature and to see Thee."[11]

[10] Thus, for example, in the Review of the religious University of Cairo, *Majallat al-Azhar* (March 1953).

[11] Cf. Part Two of *Expériences mystiques en terres non-chrétiennes,* Louis Gardet (Paris, 1953).

"No man can adore God by an act more pleasing to him than loving him", said Hallaj. And, indeed, for Hallaj it is love that gives the key to all mystery, since "in his Essence love is the Essence of essence".

Now, we have seen that the official teaching of Islam states as axiomatic that God is inaccessible. And if in its teaching of extrinsic relationship of man to God it speaks of a benevolent and merciful love of God towards the "slave", his creature, that only serves to keep more jealously closed the mystery of the intimate life of the Most High. In his "nocturnal ascent", says the tradition, the prophet Mohammed halted at the threshold of the sealed enclosure of the divine Essence. The doctors of that epoch declared that the believer can and ought to love the law of God, the commandment and the benefactions of God, but not God himself and in himself. It must be said that though Muslim law may contain the essentials of the Decalogue, it has no equivalent of the ineluctable precept of the Bible: "Thou shalt love the Lord thy God with the love of thy whole heart, and thy whole soul" (Deut. 6. 4).

And yet here were the best amongst these Sufis yearning to slake their thirst in the inaccessible depths of God. And the greatest of them understood and experienced that only love, authentic love nurtured in suffering accepted and loved, could lead them to it. In point of fact, it was towards something beyond their own explicit dogmas that they thus tended.

We can see, then, why the doctors and jurists of Islam distrusted and even opposed a way of union with God through love. They were protecting an established Community that was centered on the adoration of God the Inaccessible. No doubt the Sufi who genuinely penetrated the divine depths, and lived by that mysterious grace which "prevents" every man of upright heart, was within his rights in relying on his personal experience. But what could be the outcome when such a criterion was contested by people of lower experience? And as for the jurists, the official representatives of the established Community, how could they be expected to accept private personal experiences as the supreme rule?

Historical background

The first appearances of the Sufis did not provoke mistrust. No legal proceedings were taken against Hasan Basri who preached the constant desire for the Lord,[12] nor against Rabia with her appeal to disinterested love of God. Nor was there any opposition shown towards the all but hopeless efforts of Bistami. Twelve years, he says, he hammered his "self" on the anvil. His terrible asceticism, like Indian Yoga, was centred on the experience of absolute unity at the essential centre of the soul, a denuding of personality and an intellectual retortion and a straining after the pure "I", with neither form nor attribute, in the presence of divine Essence.

But in the third century A.H., when the selfsame theme of divine love was again predominant, Misri was persecuted in Egypt, Muhasibi was in semi-banishment at Kufa, Ibn Karram imprisoned, Tustari died in exile at Basra, Nuri cited before the tribunals with several of his disciples. And lastly, Hallaj, whatever the alleged political and "ecclesiastical" motives, was condemned, tortured and executed for having expounded the possibility of a union of love between God and his creature man, infinitely remote from each other, Eternal and contingent being.[13] His contemporaries, Junayd and Shibli, retreated into a prudent esotericism. Many later Sufis were to reproach Hallaj, not for his experience or his doctrine, but not for keeping them quietly to himself. Hallaj's scaffold still leaves Islam wondering at heart.

The secular arm took action again in the twelfth century (sixth century A.H.) against Ayn al-Qudat and Suhrawardi, the "master of illumination" (*ishraq*). In this latter case there came into the picture a wide field of gnostic doctrinal teach-

[12] As a "traditional" sentence says: "I desire him and he desires me", *hadith qudsi* understood as a fidelity to remember him, placed by God in the heart of his servant.

[13] Cf. *Diwan d'al-Hallaj*, edited by Louis Massignon (Paris, 1931).

ing, inspired by ancient Persia and Greece, which sought to achieve in one illuminating flash the ontological identity of the thinker and the thought. If, as Louis Massignon says, Suhrawardi was indeed the last of the Sufis to stand away from monism, his disciples at any rate soon crossed its threshold.

All through these first two periods of Sufism, there was a growing interest in a subtle psychological analysis of the "spiritual states": varied shades of introspection which found an admirably suitable medium of expression in the semantic genius of Arabic. To take but two examples, they range from the *Ri-aya* of Muhasibi to the *Manazil* of Ansari (eleventh century A.D.).

In the third period of Sufism, beginning with the sixth and seventh centuries A.H., we find the great writings of Ibn al-Farid, "prince of the loving", Ibn Arabi, Jalal al-Din Rumi and Abd al-Karim Jili. These works represent one of the richest legacies of Arab and Persian culture. At this period the mystics still speak of love and union through love. But it is sometimes difficult to make out whether they mean a love of charity such as, it would seem, Rabia and Hallaj postulated, or ontological love, the gravitation by which a creature of its very nature tends towards its Creator. (Hence a love which in itself is not salutary.) Such notions show traces of Plotinus and Avicenna. Natural mysticism towards the existence of self and philosophical contemplation, then, intervene with certain traditional elements retained from the great epoch of Sufism. Here care must be taken against mistaking flights of poetic genius for accounts of genuine experiences.

It was likewise in the thirteenth and fourteenth centuries that influences from the Far East were frequently felt, probably through Turko-Mongolian channels. These influences finally produced a new "technique", alleged to be mystically efficacious, combining the ancient practice of saying the divine names over and over again (*dhikr*) with physical movements. Along with all this went the gradual decadence of the "brotherhoods". It is these that the modern reformers have in mind when they take on themselves to condemn Sufism *en bloc*. But we need hardly say that it is on an entirely different plane that Islam seeks to evolve the problem of the quest for union with God.

The double stream of Muslim mysticism

That there were influences which left their mark in the course of time is undeniable. But, whatever may be thought of the alien trimmings, the problem certainly belongs to the realm of Muslim culture. Proof of that is that mystical experience first impressed the Sufis—all of them—as an inward achieving of unicity, *tawhid*. Unification of self with self, unification of self with God, unicity of God in the soul of the mystic, this triple process may be found in almost every experience recorded. however varied the means by which it sought realization. But at this point there is a parting into two great streams.

The first of these is the "unicity of witness" (*wahdat al-shuhud*), which, prevalent in the second and third centuries A.H., culminated in the experiences of Hallaj and was later resuscitated in certain Shadhili trends.[14] It seems inevitable that a mystic under Hanbalite influences, like Ansari, should aspire to this experience. The term "unicity of witness" denotes, Hallaj would say, that God bears witness to himself in his mystery within the heart of the Sufi. Divine transcendence and its absolute unicity remains at the core of formulated faith; the encounter is effected through love, a dialogue between the faithful heart and God, reaching out to the supreme "I", which, without destroying it, aims at the consummation of the dialogue in unity. It is in this context that Hallaj uses his "theopathetic locutions". They led the jurists of his day to tax him with impiety, whereas some Sufis of a

[14] A famous school of Sufism which originated in the Maghreb. One of its most outstanding exponents is Ibn Abbad of Ronda.

later age, Ibn Arabi for instance, were to deplore the "duality" (of nature) preserved between the mystic and God.[15]

That brings us to the other stream of Muslim mysticism, namely, that of "unicity of Existence" (or of Being), *wahdat al-wujud*. This was to become predominant with Ibn Arabi (sixth and seventh centuries A.H.) and, two centuries later, found expression in the "Perfect Man" of Abd al-Karim Jili, to quote but one example. Ibn Taymiyya quite rightly detects in it the neo-Platonist influence of Avicenna, though his account of it seems to lack precision. It was foreshadowed by Ghazali in the opuscula written towards the end of his life and still more by certain gnoses of the *Ishraq*.

In this second stream there is a paradoxical combining of the Plotinian monism of the pseudo-*Theology of Aristotle* and the Asharite statement of God the only Being and the only Agent. The contingent world, the mystic will say, is merely a manifested reflection of the one divine Existence and the human spirit merely a direct manifestation of uncreated Essence. Empirical existence has thus no depth of being, no ontological consistency. It is an existence which has to reduce itself to nothing (*fana*) in God who alone abides (*baqa*). We have here an echo, though in a different context, of the "vestige of the One" in us of which Plotinus speaks, or, leaving aside the question of its historical derivation, an echo of the Identity encountered in Indian mysticism: *atman* (self) is *brahman* (trans-personal Absolute). Mystical union will thus be conceived as an identification (*ittihad*) in which the personality of the Sufi is absorbed and volatilized in *one* Absolute called God.

The "unicity of being" was the quarry that lured both gnosis and ascetical techniques, and both were constantly current in Muslim mysticism. That is clear in the lines of the great poet Ibn al-Farid: "The greeting I give him is a pure metaphor: in reality it is from me to Me that my salutation goes." Or: "... and it is by my own gift that my soul is

[15] Ibn Arabi was, of course, a pantheist.

repleted"; or again, the words, so Hallaj claimed, addressed to him by God:

"I have embraced with my whole being thy love, O my holiness! Thou hast manifested thyself in me in such guise that it seems forsooth thyself art in me".

Quite certainly the Sufism of Hallaj was not historically the predominant characteristic of the religious climate of Islam. But it does remain the highest expression of that climate and the ultimate question aroused in the heart of "believers" by the desire to penetrate the Word of God. It must be remembered that the best among the Sufis turned instinctively towards Christ—the Christ portrayed explicitly in the Koran—as to the supreme model of sanctity, and that a man like Ibn Arabi, despite the fact that his monist formulas introduced a criss-cross of natural and supernatural mysticism into his work, took as his supreme rule the rule of life of Christ.

CHAPTER VI

CULTURE AND HUMANISM

THE LEGACY OF ISLAM

The various Islamic sciences, from the very first to the sixth century A.H., produced many great works. Some of them were readily given a place in universal culture, though, it may be contended, not as generally as they deserved, the main obstacle being that their scope is so specifically Islamic. Better known are the literary works, prose and poetry, of Muslim mysticism. These are readily available to Western readers.

But perhaps more than anything else it is the profane arts and sciences of Islam and its religious architecture and associated arts that have attracted most attention from non-Muslim countries at the present day. Here the first place must be given to literature (*adab*). There are the famous poems of the Umayyad court by such poets as Jarir, Akhtal and Farazdaq.[1] Still more famous perhaps are the poems of Abu Nuwas, the "libertine", a familiar of the court of Harun al-Rashid and a convert late in life. Then, a little later, there is Abu al-Atahiya and Abu al-Maarri, austere and solitary, somewhat suspect of unorthodox views, the poet of the pathos of life and death. Prose-writing was particularly brilliant under the Abbasids with, among many others, Jahiz, the Mutazilite, and Hamadhani in Sijistan and Hariri at Basra, whose "séances" (*maqamat*) in rhythmic prose may well be regarded as the distant forerunners of the modern novel. It would be impossible to attempt here a selection of even the greatest names in

[1] Jarir the Beduin, Akhtal the Jacobite Christian, Farazdaq the redoubtable satirist.

classical Arabic literature, with its perfection of form, but with themes, too often modelled on an inflexible pattern and erotic or Bacchic in content, which were taken up over and over again in works of a more popular texture—the poets and story-tellers of *suqs* and public squares, the *Fool of Layla*, the *Romance of Antar*, the fables of Lukham, Sinbad the Sailor and the *Thousand and One Nights*.

Despite the opposition of the doctors of the law to profane art, an abundance of musicians, singers and dancers made their appearance in the Umayyad and Abbasid courts of the East and, in the West, in the caliphate of Cordova and Granada and Seville and in many more or less autonomous sultanates. The prohibition against reproducing the human form in art, or for that matter any living being, was respected in the decoration of the mosques but in no way prevented the creation of Persian miniatures nor the admirable output of ceramic art. But this had its beginnings in the wonderful tracery of the capitals and walls of the mosques and, for instance, the Tombs of the Caliphs in Cairo. The best examples are the Hispano-Muslim arabesques.[2]

The skill of the architects in devising their ground-plans and balancing their masses was unsurpassed. Amongst famous works are the palace of Samarra, the Umayyad mosque at Damascus and those of Ibn Tulun and al-Azhar in Cairo, the cupola of Umar and the al-Aqsa mosque in Jerusalem, the Alhambra in Cordova, the Mosque of the Pearl in Delhi, the Taj Mahal at Agra. But there is no end to the list of buildings that rank amongst the finest achievements of religious and secular architecture in the world.

Special mention should be made of the lay-out of gardens, all converging to the centre, with their ornamental fountains and basins.

[2] The story is told of a Persian artist converted to Islam who was distressed at having to give up his art. "Come, come," said the Caliph Umar II, "disguise your human figures as flowers and then cut off their heads."

It must be remembered, also, that the development of mathematics, astronomy, medicine and pharmacology in Islam was several centuries in advance of the Latin Middle Ages. Furthermore, the *falsafa*, which we have already encountered, the Arab-Muslim or Irano-Muslim philosophy of Hellenic inspiration, afforded Christian scholars of the thirteenth century the benefit of its well-tried structure as well as—for good or ill—its conception of synthesis. The records kept by Muslim travellers and geographers are also precious documents. The historians, it is true, were hardly more than chroniclers, but their information is precise and well substantiated. And besides, in the fourteenth century, just before Muslim culture entered its uncreative era, the sociologist Ibn Khaldun did work that foreshadowed the modern scientific methods of historical scholarship.

Thus profane Arab-Muslim and Persian-Muslim culture, and later and in a lesser degree Turko-Muslim culture, handed on a real legacy to the culture of the West. It is quite possible that a great deal of that legacy has still to be turned to good account. How far it will be integrated in the universal culture of tomorrow will depend, it would seem, on the results of the "reawakening" (*nahda*) which has been taking place in Islamic countries since the end of the nineteenth century and on whether or not Islam recaptures its past capacity for creative work.

CLASSICAL HUMANISM

The problem of humanism

Is there such a thing as Muslim humanism? If we take a very broad definition of humanism, we may say that humanist culture is every culture that recognizes in man a being of exceptional worth and encourages him to develop his profound and latent productivity.

Hence, one may be tempted to see evidence of Arab (or Persian) humanism in the intellectual and gnostic trends which set out to cultivate the prototype or myths of the "perfect man" (*al-insan al-kamil*), for do they not exhibit an absolute confidence in the unlimited capacity for progress in the human reason illumined by the "angelic" world of intelligibilia? It would be difficult to draw up a list of names in this connection, for it is not so much a matter of a clearly defined school of thought as of trends of thought appearing spasmodically. We may, however, mention the gnostic Jafar, the doctor of medicine, Abu Bakr al-Razi (known to the Middle Ages as Razes), some passages from the Mutazalite Jahiz, the extremist Sufi Abd al-Karim Jili. In these writers reference to one God, creator, remunerator, frequently lacks clear definition. Their concept of man may vary considerably, but they are quite content to leave him in a purely material sphere.

It is well to remember that this tendency, so virulent in the present-day dechristianized West, has not been unknown in Islam. But it was not a universal tendency. For it is clear that any religion professing that man has an eternal and individual destiny must necessarily demand respect for that destiny during man's lifetime on earth. And, indeed, Islam does manifest this respect in regard to every believer. We may add that Islam also owes it to itself to profess this respect in regard to all human beings as potential servants of God.

Undoubtedly, the emphasis placed on the transcendence of the Creator postulates a corresponding emphasis on the vacuity of the creature: "Everything shall perish except (God) himself" (Koran, 28, 88). Nevertheless, in the specifically Muslim notions, we find many allusions to the human person (*shakhs*) as a witness to God, to the use of the reason which must "reflect on the signs of the universe", says the Koran, and to the interior liberation of man "surrendered" (*muslim*) to God. It would be difficult not to see in all this a possible starting-point for humanism.

Does history record any achievements in this direction? It

most certainly does. But one would hesitate to say that all the resources have been fully exploited. That, however, is proof that Muslim humanism is not merely a thing of the past but has still much to give if only it awakens to its latent potentialities and devotes its energies to their realization.

Basic elements

Wherever humanism comes into being it is always associated with a culture. In the past, three chief elements went into the making of Muslim humanism. We have already met them. The basis for future achievements can be foreseen to include the psychological traits and the social trends of Arab life, the inborn attraction of the Arab race for poetry and eloquence and two other of their tendencies—each corroborating the other rather than excluding it—namely, an individualism which is readily on the defensive and a firm attachment to the traditional pattern of life. Arab-Muslim culture has always had a marked capacity for absorbing concepts from outside sources. In this it has been admirably served by the Arabic tongue with its wealth of expression and its art of embodying varied shades of meaning in elegance of form. Then also there is the richness and courtesy of Arab hospitality, a virtue very dear to them, and their sense of loyalty and respect for their word of honour.

Secondly, Muslim humanism found in Greek culture a veritable life-stream. This came about in two ways. Firstly, the people of the Near East who were converted to Islam or lived amongst the Muslims were steeped in Byzantine-Syriac Christian culture; hence Islam's direct contact with it, for these people brought with them the ethos of Byzantium—basilican architecture, Byzantine law and system of government—into the very life of the Arab Empire of the Umayyads. There is scope for a great deal of study on the transition in architecture from the basilica to the mosque and in law from Byzantine law to Koranic law.

The second source of influence is this. From the time of the Abbasids, a great intellectual invasion took place under the patronage of the caliphs in the form of translations of the philosophical and scientific works of antiquity. Thus Islam inherited the thought of ancient Greece, though, strangely enough, not nearly so much its literary legacy. It was thus that, one after another, libraries sprang up to house these works on "alien" sciences. Such a thirst for knowledge of the culture of past ages and such eagerness for its revival was not to be seen in the West until the fifteenth and sixteenth centuries.

Lastly, starting once more in the time of the Abbasids, the people of Islam became fascinated by Persian literature and art and even by some Persian religious traditions. Traces of this are found as far afield as Andalusia. We may quote, for instance, the music of which the court of the caliph was so fond and the importance given in the *Kitab al-Aghani* to the songs of the third century A.H. and the composers, singers and dancers of the period. Besides this, the philosophical and cultural encyclopaedia of the "Sincere Brethren" (*Ikhwan al-Safa*) gave considerable space to musical theories in which the influence of Persia and that of Pythagorean Greece are both in evidence.

All this was needed to bring into existence classical Arab music with its characteristic melodic embellishments. A further enrichment was to come through Andalusia, for the musician and aesthetic, Zriyab, pupil of the famous Mawsili of the East, left Baghdad and settled at the court of the great patron of literature and art, al-Rahman II, the Umayyad caliph of Spain.

The same influences played their parts in every branch of artistic productivity. There is a distinction, however, to be made. The outside influences were felt mostly in secular architecture, music and the secondary arts, whereas literature, both prose and poetry, preserved more fully the stamp of its Beduin origins, going back to Arabia of long before.

The architecture and embellishments of the mosques had this about them that, notwithstanding the influence of the Christian, Persian and Mongol strains of Byzantine art, they achieved a variety of original styles, all, however, bearing a common trait marking them for their Muslim religious purpose.

Humanism at the court

The great epochs of classical humanism coincide with the periods when culture was at its zenith.[3] We have listed them already. But the earliest manifestation is a humanism somewhat after the manner of the sixteenth century, whose favourite diversion was tilting at religious prescriptions and observances. This was a brilliant and even refined humanism, at least under the Abbasids and in Andalusia, but tainted with the licence of the court and dependent on the patronage of sovereigns. Rare indeed were the poets, artists or philosophers who, like Abu 'l-Ala al-Maari, fled the court more than they attended it. It was a humanism for fashionable folk with plenty of time on their hands, who had mastered the art of extracting from life its full content of pleasure and were all too ready to welcome a powerfully profane philosophy and literature with something of the same proclivity they showed for wines and games and fine silks and paintings and that subtly intoxicating music of Andalusia. Official teaching frowned on them or condemned them. The general impression is of an atmosphere of elegant luxury redolent of a craze for perfection of form. In odes and snatches of love songs, the *ghazal* and the lyrical flights of the *qasida*[4] with

[3] See Umayyad Empire, Chapter II, above.

[4] The *qasida* is a poem of considerable length. Its original structure illustrates the minute concern for form in Muslim literature. The same rhyme and metre ran right through the poem. There was a set plan for every *qasida*. First came the *nasib* or introduction of a romantic kind in which the poet describes how he went to see his beloved, only to find the camp had moved, and gives vent to his despair. Then comes a description of his journey to the habitation

their occasional breath of the epic, or again, in the famous rhythmic prose of the *maqamat*—everywhere, perfection of form.

This humanism might almost be called aristocratic. But not in the sense of belonging to a caste: such a thing would be alien to Islam. A fair number of the literary folk about the court came from what could be called the middle classes, others were of still more modest origins. And if they thus found their way into high society, they owed it entirely to their talent and ability and the patronage of their sovereign. Thus for instance Ibn Abi Amir, who was a poor scholar at Cordova and became the famous Mansur Billah—known to the Latin West as Almanzor. Although this humanism belonged to the court, it had its repercussions on the townsfolk, and the scholars and jurists of the mosques and madrasah made it their concern, if only to counteract its licentiousness. And, at least in the early days, when intellectual and artistic controversy ran too high, the townsfolk were quick to have their say. The *Book of Songs* (*Kitab al-Aghani*) tells of the Umayyad army enthusing over poetry and hotly debating the relative merits of the poems of Jarir and Farazdaq. Subsequently, a real culture, though of a coarser grain, existed amongst the trade and merchant guilds. Thus there are works in more popular language and texture such as the *mawwal* of Baghdad, written in dialectic Arabic and *zajal* and *muwasha* from Andalusia and Maghreb, which owe their fame to the wandering bard Ibn Qusman and the Sufi Shushtari.

On more than one occasion the guardians of religious

---

of those whom he intends to praise. This gives the poet ample scope to describe the terrors of the desert and to compare his camel with various desert animals. And lastly comes the main section of the poem which contains his praise—or insult—of the person or tribe he has in view. Some poets sometimes ended with drawing a moral. This literary form never lost the stamp of its pre-Islamic Beduin origins. Sometimes, however, a certain amount of liberty was taken in the choice of subjects.

tradition had to assume an anti-humanist rôle: for poets, artists, pseudo-Sufis and philosophers vied with one another in disregarding the accepted moral code. To see the Abbasid epoch in its true perspective one has only to reconstruct the vivid and alarming picture of the life of the élite of Baghdad, drawn for us by the Hanifite jurist and anti-mystic Tanukhi.

All the same, it would be just as wrong to think that all Muslim humanists were free-thinkers as to identify the "libertines" and free-thinkers of the present day with Christian humanism. For one thing, there never was in Islam the sort of segregation of humanism and religion that existed in Renaissance Europe. And besides, the influence of Muslim ascetical and even mystical writers never ceased to be felt. Sufism, in its early stages, more than once caused a stir in the world of letters. Works as outstanding as those of Husan Basri, to mention but one author, spread the concepts of return to God, relinquishment and renunciation. The free-thinkers, by and large, remained genuine Muslims. To enjoy life, knowing all the time that one is not compromised in any essentials, is only another way of expressing one's belief in the vacuity of creatures! To turn from the enjoyment of creatures to renunciation is, by the same token, a matter of the heart rather than of the intellect. The Beduin poet, Jarir, earned Umar II's patronage by his reputation for piety and chastity. There were princes who became ascetics. It is said that Abu Nuwas was converted to detachment in his old age despite the efforts of Harun al-Rashid to dissuade him, and it was perhaps through his ascetical poems—of a rather unorthodox syncretist trend, it should be said—that Abu 'l-Atayiha owed the best of his reputation.

So it comes to this: this brilliant classical humanism, nothing loath to antagonize Islam of the strict observance, became impregnated with the Muslim outlook and values by sheer contact with them; and, by the same token, traditional Islam could not fail to absorb some of the beauty and undoubted acquisitions of literature, art and profane sciences which that humanism produced. Western culture knew all too little of them or knew them in a distorted form, and its only real gain from them were certain philosophical elements, with which it became acquainted through twelfth-century Latin translations, and some lyrical or romantic works, such as the *Romance of Antar* and the *Thousand and One Nights*. It is high time that many other Muslim works of outstanding quality were acclimatized to universal culture.[5]

WHAT OF THE FUTURE?

We have already suggested that the potentialities of Muslim humanism are far from being exhausted. To be precise one should speak of a past humanist culture, one, indeed, of the most brilliant ever known to history, rather than of a humanism properly so called.

The concept of man and of human liberty which we postulated above are quite certainly loftier notions than those propounded by the kind of humanism that existed in the Muslim palace and court. For these, moral licence was often paraded as liberty, as though the vacuity of creatures could only be compensated by a quest for perfection of form and indulgence in pleasures immediately to hand. Besides, this humanism was often stifled by the people—the half-literate townspeople and the illiterate country folk. Nevertheless, the people were faithful to the traditional virtues of hospitality and mutual aid, they practised confident resignation in the hands of God—though a rather too inert resignation on occasion—they had a wealth of folklore and of story-tellers and preachers, and all this, in their lives, added up to the makings of a future humanism.

This estrangement of the people was perhaps one of the obstacles to the revival of culture during the centuries of

[5] UNESCO is sponsoring various translations of such works.

torpor under the Ottoman domination. Culture just about managed to survive—a manual here, a gloss there—but it made hardly any discernible progress.

In the nineteenth century the revival came. It was then that the people of Islam awakened to their own worth. They came face to face with modern Western civilization and its enormous economic and technical progress. They also encountered Western designs for domination and they themselves were all too often a stake in international politics. It was a rude awakening. At the time of the Abbasids—all Islam preserves a vivid remembrance of those times—Baghdad was above all others the city of civilization, and Europe was still in a primitive state. By the end of the nineteenth century Europe looked patronizingly on Muslim civilization as a survival of the Middle Ages.

There was an anti-humanist bent and over-reliance on interior values, patience and the disposition to leave everything to God. But Arab thought preserved its vast receptivity, all the more so for having been left fallow so long. It was just as infatuated by Western civilization as the ninth-century Abbasids had been by Greek thought. The translations of European and American books are now as abundant as the translations of Greek and Syriac works were in those days. The result has been an output of new literary work by Christian and Muslim Arabs, who have succeeded in harnessing the riches of Arabic to the creation of new work. New fields, like the theatre and the novel—hardly, if ever, used before—have been opened.

But this fascination by Western thought is all too indiscriminate—it is not always stimulated by what is best. The selection is less enlightened than that made by the Baghdad translators of Greek thought. It is dechristianized, materialistic Western thought that is often made accessible to the peoples of Islam. So much so, that they freely condemn Western thought and reject it, though they are inevitably influenced by it, even by the elements in it which they find most objectionable. The greatest seduction to which the young Muslim intellectual is at present subjected is dialectical materialism. The translations of the works of Karl Marx, Lenin and Mao-Tse-Tung, have been in great demand. People who read them forget the purely Western origin of Marxism—the full circle of the dechristianization of the modern world—and only look for an immediately workable political economic framework. There is here a grave danger, far more serious than the danger incurred at the time of the "libertines", the *zanadiqa* of the past.

Here, then, is the urgent question regarding the future of Muslim culture and humanism: will it be caught up by the efficiency and power of a dechristianized West or will it prove itself capable of grasping a universal and elevated sense of man, whose true greatness is first and foremost in his being an intelligent and free creature in the hands of God the Merciful?

CHAPTER VII[1]

ISLAM TODAY

MAIN TRENDS

We have already encountered what has been termed the "reawakening" (*nahda*) of Islam. In the case of most Muslim countries, independence will mean a transition from a feudal or quasi-feudal system to one of modern structure, and that within the space of a few years. Two alternative patterns are before them. One is nationalism on Western lines, secularized or with a policy tending to secularization, in which the legislator would be at liberty to modify traditional law as he thought fit and in which religion would be entirely a personal matter for each individual, with no place whatever in the life of the State. A typical example of this is the Kemal revolution in Turkey. The same ideal is proposed in the works of Ali Abd al-Raziq and more recently those of Qasimi and the Shaykh Khalid in Egypt and again in the movement launched by Haddad in Tunisia in 1933.

The other alternative is again nationalism. But this time, instead of simply copying European penal and civil codes, Islam would be integrated into the administrative life of the country, and the fundamental principle of Muslim teaching would provide a basis for a sincerely religious commonwealth capable of absorbing and developing the discoveries of modern technology. This is the ideal of the "orthodox reformists," the *salafiyya*, who revere the "Ancients" and the sources of pure Islam freed from superstitious accretions and the stultifying juridical rigorism of past centuries. Launched

[1] Events move so rapidly that it has not been possible to keep up to date in the treatment of the political background to Chapters VII and VIII.

in the nineteenth century by Afghani and the famous Mohammed Abduh—though some of Abduh's disciples were very near being secularists—this movement gained ground with Rashid Rida and his review *Manar*. An extremist and activist form of it can be found with the Muslim Brotherhood. Nowadays it would seem that a less rigid "reformism" is being sought.

While it is never quite satisfactory to set down such classifications, we would not hesitate to place Muslim countries today in three groups.

Predominantly traditionalist

The feudal structure is predominant, though superficially modernized in Afghanistan, for example, or in the Emirates, which are independent although economically subjugated—thus Oman, Kuwait, Bahrain. Moreover, one still finds a feudal system in operation in countries which have already determined their progressive programme, as for example Jordan. Indeed, in recent years in Jordan, in the tension between the king and the people, the patriarchal organization of the Jordan tribes made itself very much felt. Iran, by religion Shiite, has long since had a parliament and all the machinery of democratic government and yet is very far from having integrated the social and economic framework of their traditional way of life. In the case of Morocco, the central government has set out to absorb into one unified and modernized structure such traces of feudalism as still survive.

The old religious brotherhoods, which are in one way or another a degraded form of Sufism, long persisted as the spiritual framework, as it were, of the economic and social structures of bygone days. They came to terms on more than one occasion with foreign elements, they produced forms of religious nationalism, culminating in the nineteenth century with the Sanusi Kingdom, reviving the temporal eschatology of the old Mahdist dream. Waiting for the

Mahdi, the restorer of Islam at the end of time and the precursor of the day of judgement, was the leading idea of many popular movements.[2] It has now lost its appeal and other more modern forms of nationalism have taken its place. The part played by the brotherhoods, and indeed their very existence, is steadily declining.

The Saudi Kingdom of Arabia, which has been in evidence in the political arena for some decades, calls for special mention. Taking the principles on which it has been acting, it might be considered as the forerunner of the third group about which we shall presently speak. But the actual picture it presents places it with the predominantly traditionalist countries. Its particular "reform" consisted in adopting the theocratic principle of the Wahhabites, the eighteenth-century school of thought which set out to revive Islam as it was originally, divested of all the superstitious accretions and therefore of all religious brotherhoods. Hence its marked fidelity to the smallest detail of Koranic prescriptions. Thus it is that, far from turning to Europe for a model penal or civil code, Saudi Arabia sets out to apply the penalties (*hudud*) inflicted by Muslim Law. The thief must have his hand cut off,[3] the adulterer must be stoned, etc.[4]

In this century Abd al-Aziz Ibn Saud succeeded in quelling the anarchy of the tribes. Having perceived that modern technology did not involve any specific moral commitments, he set out to give his country the benefits of modern discoveries. He turned the élite of the Beduins into a sedentary people and gave them machinery. He allowed American prospectors in to exploit petroleum, and the riches brought to the royal treasury by Aramco are no secret.

In between the two World Wars, the "orthodox reformists" in Islam looked hopefully towards Saudi Arabia as to

[2] The position of Mahdism in present-day trends in Islam has been ably studied by H. A. R. Gibb in *Modern Trends in Islam* (1947), University of Chicago Press.

[3] Koran, 5, 38. [4] *Ibid.*, 24, 2.

a country which embodied the discoveries of science in an absolute fidelity to the politico-religious laws of the Koran. When Rashid Rida and his Salafi movement came to grief in Egypt, it was to Riyadh that he turned for hospitality.

However, the Saudi family did not really alter the tribal and feudal basis of the country. At the present day Arabia presents a paradox: a State that has adopted modern technical progress and yet is governed by the reigning family on out-of-date lines. There is an immense discrepancy between the wealth and way of living of the chiefs and the poverty, in money and means, of their subjects. One picture symbolizes the situation—television and luxury cars alongside the Beduin tents. Meantime Aramco is training skilled labour and Arab technicians. Young men are being sent to foreign universities, particularly in America. The day can be foreseen when the Wahhabist theories of officialdom, which are already commanding less fervour even amongst its supporters, will clash with ambitions and revindications which have gone unsatisfied.

This discrepancy between the lives of the chiefs and the people, in so far as it is subordinated to an alien economy, is certainly a handicap to the evolution of Arabia. It is no longer the leader it was in the eyes of the reformists. It seems now to bear more resemblance to the United Arab Republic and the United Arab States.

Secularist trends

The Muslim States which were independent or nearly independent immediately after the First World War, first took the pattern of their new organizations from Europe. Hence their story is that of the impact of secularist trends on specifically Muslim solutions and opinions. How much each of these two ingredients has been used varies from country to country and even within each nation, according to the policy of successive parties in power.

Kemal Ataturk's reform and his spectacular suppression

of the Ottoman caliphate was entirely secularist. Ever since 1924, despite reformist projects and the "Caliphate Congress", the Muslim world has been without a supreme imam at its head in so far as its religious Law is concerned. The *umma*, for all that, remains a reality as a Community, but it is still looking for some device to hold it together. The Turkish Republic, however, stands as the extreme example of the predominantly Muslim secularized State. The youthful Indonesian State is secularist but acknowledges the existence of God.

Secularist trends in most Arab countries (the Syro-Egyptian Republic and Iraq with their "Arab nationalism", Tunisia with its own particular policy) present a different picture altogether. The Lebanon is in a separate category with its equality of treatment for different religions.

The ideals of the United Arab States make an ever stronger appeal to popular sentiment. From the time of its revolution in July 1958, Iraq seemed destined to be one of its chief promoters. At present, Egypt and Syria are its leaders. In February 1958 the member States became the United Arab Republic with Gamal Abd al-Nasser as its president. The men responsible for this aim at making it the beginnings of an Arab nation.

For our present purpose we may note that, in outlook more even than in declared policy, Syria is clearly more secularized than Egypt. Both were influenced by various European codes. But in its previous constitutions, Egypt declared itself an Arab country of Muslim religion, whereas in Syria, Islam was simply the religion of the majority and the President of the Syrian Republic had to be a Muslim. These countries found themselves a stake in the policies of East and West, and the U.S.S.R. was thus able to offer them economic aid as a contribution to Arab independence. The furtherance of that independence in regard to both East and West is the predominant aim of the United Republic. But Islam no longer enters into its definition: everything is focused on Arabism and its traditional urge for power.[5] The United Republic calls on all Arab countries to join in a wide federation and President Nasser has not disguised his dream of complete homogeneity. The Yemen was the first State to become a member, without sacrificing its autonomy or its own monarchy. The notion of State authority has taken the place of Parliamentary democracy. Whether the "Arab Nation" will succumb to the temptation of a Fascist type of government, seek to further its interests by more or less deliberately provoking "racism" or take a comprehensive view of Islam as a starting-point and thence contrive successfully to side-step both Fascism and racism—both *ersatz* products of the West—remains to be seen.

The evolution of Arab countries brings up the question of minorities in an acute form. In each country there are Jewish and Christian minority groups of varying sizes. The United Arab Republic has declared that all citizens are equal whatever their religion. But despite the provisions of the laws and constitutions, real equality between Muslim and non-Muslim is rarely found in practice. Syria was the country where this equality was best observed. It would be difficult to say the same of the others. It may be due to some remnant of religious fanaticism or to incomplete secularization but is more likely the result of lurking suspicion of the Christian minorities; suspicion of them is more marked in places where in the past they themselves were more apprehensive about intolerance. The problem is a complex one. During the struggle for independence, the number of Arab Christians who took part in pro-nationalist activities was relatively large.

The subordination of the temporal to the spiritual, which Christianity teaches, formed no part of their patriotic sentiments: they thought rather in terms of an absolute separation

[5] The Provisional Constitution, signed by General Nasser and Kwatly on February 1st, 1958, and ratified by the Egyptian and Syrian parliaments on February 5th, 1958, says: "The United Arab State is a democratic, independent and sovereign republic. Its people belong to the Arab Nation."

of the two, after the manner of nineteenth-century Europe. Whatever may have been done in the past, when religion was in the very marrow of public life, they took it for granted that the new State would take a neutral stand towards religion while protecting full religious liberty, and that only the *jus loci* would function. But the majority of the Arab Muslims instinctively thought of religion, blood and soil as one thing. Even today it is still true to say that, to an Arab, Muslim means totally Arab and that it is only on those grounds that a right to citizenship exists.

This outlook is not so much a religious sentiment as the product of the people's history and social life. We feel safe in saying that this is less marked in Syria than in Egypt. The nationalist party in Syria brought about the union with Egypt and provided the framework of the single party, *al-bath al-arabi* (the Arab revival), and it counts many Christians among its militants. The Muslim élite at Damascus is often secularist: it is familiar with Western culture and was brought up on French culture. Perhaps tomorrow it will be the turn of Soviet culture. It thinks "Arab"—often with a real indifference to religion—and no longer "Muslim".

The evolution of Egypt took place in two distinct phases. The first phase was an attempt at a constitutional monarchy after the British pattern; the then nationalist party (the Wafd) did not allow religious discrimination. This was formal, though not social, democracy, and it led up to the crises in 1951 and to the seizure of power by the "officers of the revolution". The setting up of the consortium of officers to the exclusion of General Neguib was favourable to the dictatorial régime of Abd al-Nasser, who appeared to the mass of the Arab peoples outside Egypt as the promoter of their total independence and renewed power.

At its source, the Egyptian revolution was a national affair. It has since become linked with the myth of Arabism, which is primarily concerned with community of race, it can be said perhaps, of spiritual race. In any case, the underlying principles of the revolution were not expressed in terms of religion. But the "officers of the revolution" are Muslims. There are no Christians among them as there are among the militants in Syria. The Syrian élite is acquainted with Western thought. The Egyptian "officers" have little knowledge of European languages and still less, it would seem, of the place occupied by the West in history and culture. Undoubtedly they would be quite prepared to waive many of the traditional rules of Islam and they proclaim that the Christians of Egypt are their fellow citizens. But by the very fact that "spiritual racism" is so intimate a part of the motive force of Arabism in its extreme form, they do not find it easy to give Christian minorities their unreserved confidence. Hence the present uneasiness of the Christians of Egypt: they fear that their civic and political rights are not sufficiently guaranteed. Each year, especially since 1957, two or three thousand Orthodox Copts go over to Islam—thus opening the door to their social betterment.

In any case, while Turkey thought of its independence in terms of specifically national ideals, Egypt and Syria, once they became the United Republic, began to think of their political evolution in terms of the "Arab Nation" as such. Secularization in the modern sense suddenly finds itself in line with the Umayyad Arab Empire, more directly perhaps than with the Muslim unity of Salah al-Din (Saladin) with whom Nasser once claimed affinity.

Special mention must be made of Tunisia, which took forthright steps to remodel its statutes (suppression of polygamy, etc.) and proclaimed its loyalty to Arabism, while refusing to become involved in Syro-Egyptian politics. More "secularist" than "reformist", Tunisia for all that invokes principles borrowed from the Salafiyyas to justify its most radical measures.

"Reformist" perspectives

We put forward this third group as a pure hypothesis. It would comprise Muslim States who want to remain as such and would reject Western secularism and work out constitutive principles on the basis of the "rights of God and of man" and not only the "rights of man" as in nineteenth-century Europe. As far as can be made out at present, the extreme east and the extreme west—non-Arab Pakistan on the one hand, and Arab and Arabized Morocco on the other—seem likely to follow this path.

This is not a matter of compromise with the traditional (feudal) trends. Quite the contrary. A secularized State may for a time tolerate survivals of an outmoded way of life, out of conviction that they will sooner or later be absorbed. A Muslim "reformed" State owes it to itself to undertake forthwith the education of its people and in particular the adaptation of its rural and nomadic population to the new economic pattern. A secularized State will often exact the necessary evolution in establishing a central administrative system. A "reformed" State, if it intends to protect and enlighten the religious outlook of its people, must devise its social and economic measures in keeping with higher ideals in which the eternal destiny of the citizen is involved. This is no easy task and it is all the more exacting because of the fusion of the spiritual and temporal in Islam. But if it is not done, then the modern structure which is harnessed to economic efficiency and output, will soon sweep all else away.

Some extremists in Pakistan once advocated a "Koranic State" in which the only law recognized would be the Muslim *jus religionis* and its egalitarian theocracy. Modified and more moderate trends have prevailed and they perhaps are explained by the presence of many Shiite elements and various heterodox sects within the Sunnite mass of the population. Muhammad Iqbal[6] stands out as the great precursor in this field. Pakistan has declared itself an Islamic republic and a member of the British Commonwealth. But there are still marked differences, and even opposition, between the West of Pakistan, which stands by the reformist principles and speaks Urdu, and the East, whose language

[6] Cf. Cantwell Smith, *Modern Islam in India* (Lahore 1943).

and culture are Bengali and where Islam is more traditional and more "Indianized".[7]

This reformist trend which we have been trying to define seems to be one of the elements in the evolution of present-day Morocco. The penal and civil codes now being worked out are not simply a copy of Western codes but will incorporate elements from the *fiqh* suited to the needs of modern life. There is in particular a clear reference to the religious law (*shar*) in regard to personal status. The works of the Istiqlal leader, Allal al-Fasi, are in keeping with views of the Salafiyya reformists.

A modernized economy on communal lines is being worked out. It remains true, however, that the capitalist economics of Western countries control the supply of the necessary technical and industrial equipment.

The principle regarding non-Muslim minorities is, or will be, an acute problem for these reformed Muslim States. The principle must be that all the inhabitants of a country are citizens with equal civic rights and duties. But while a State with secularist tendencies will integrate its minority groups on the basis of their non-Muslim codes, the reformed States will have to find a way of establishing this new equality within a framework which, throughout its history, has denied that equality. The line taken in solving this problem is rather towards the use of *ijtihad*—the free personal effort of the legislator to devise a pattern of life into which diverse groups will fit. It does not seem that such a pattern is fundamentally inconsistent with Islamic principles. The situation that happened to exist at the time of the Umayyads and Abbasids is one thing, quite another the elucidation (*istinbat*) of the few basic principles of civic life laid down by the Koran—and very few they are indeed. If something of this kind were achieved it would be the one great contribution made to Islam by the modern reformist movement.

[7] Contrary to the principles of Islam, something of the old caste system is, in practice, maintained.

CHAPTER VIII

PRESENT-DAY PROBLEMS FOR ISLAM

In this chapter we deal with some of the more urgent questions with which, it would seem, Islam is faced.

NATIONALISM

The peoples of Islam, lying dormant beneath the Ottoman sword, were meanwhile invaded in a large degree by Europe. They have now been awakened, not so much by a religious revival, as by the call of Western nationalism on a modern pattern. And on awakening, they have grown conscious of their past glories and of a sense of humiliation at finding that so many of their lands are colonies or protectorates. They are embittered, too, at seeing the comparison between their unaltered medieval style of life and the impressive technical achievements of the great powers of today. They who were once at the head of the civilized world are now, by comparison with the West, ranked amongst the underdeveloped peoples.

As a result, they have a sense of fellowship with all the Asian and African countries which have recently become independent, even with those not "people of the Book" and with whom, therefore, in times gone by, traditional law would have barred all alliance. Here is an Afro-Asian solidarity, in the spirit of Bandung, which will surely be one of the important factors in the world of tomorrow. The first cry is for independence, not only politically but economically. The Cairo meeting at the end of December 1957, which was attended by fifty-two nations, has all the appearance of a sequel to Bandung, with this difference, that it was representative of peoples and not a conference of official government delegates. It set out to be something more than a passing encounter and it devised a permanent machinery in Cairo. "Revolutionary" Egypt aimed at the leadership not only of the Arab peoples, and thence all Muslim peoples, but also of the underdeveloped countries as a whole.

The psychology of the Muslims, especially the Arab Muslims, can only be grasped if their deep-seated sense of wounded pride is borne in mind. It is their consciousness of belonging to Islam and still more of belonging to the Arab race that arouses, from the hidden depths of their age-old inheritance, this indomitable urge for independence. In the eyes of traditional Muslim law, domination of even a tiny part of the *umma*, the Muslim Community as such, is a state of "violence": only circumstances quite beyond their control can make such a situation admissible, and even then it is to be tolerated for as short a time as possible.

Along with this the Muslims have learnt, from the example of the West, to transform man's natural attachment to his country into an aggressive nationalism. The Muslim countries have struggled for independence, and will undoubtedly continue to do so, both in the name of Islam's need of political autonomy and in the name of the modern principle of the "rights of every people to decide their own fate".

At this point we once again encounter the complex situation of the intermediary communities living within the *umma*. It is a case that is constantly recurring in Islam. Each of the non-Arab or non-Arabized peoples sets itself up as an independent nation (Turkey, Indonesia, Pakistan) and the degree of solidarity with the Muslim world which each of them retains, varies with the measure in which Islam has left its mark on its social and administrative structure. But the

Arab or Arabized peoples place not only Arab solidarity but Arab unity in the forefront of their political aims. This has been the *leitmotif* of the union of Egypt and Syria, and Iraq took it as the principle of its revolutionary Republic. It is on this Arab dynamism that the mass of the people pin their hopes. It is in the name of this unity that Syro-Egyptian "active neutrality" took its stand and curbed the pro-Western trends of the governments of other countries. Muslim and Arab thus share the same destiny.

Morocco and Tunisia are members of the Arab League. But it is quite possible that the Maghreb as a whole, though inevitably involved in Arab unity, may well interpret it in a way that does not imply political subservience and may pay its allegiance only to the spiritual issues of Islam. If on this classification a distinction of nationalist trends is to be made, it can be said that Pakistan thinks of itself as Muslim, Morocco thinks of itself as Arab Muslim and Syria thinks of itself as primarily Arab and secondarily Muslim. In the light of this trend, it can readily be understood that absorption in a large and powerful unit made a stronger appeal to Syria than a precarious existence as a State with purely artificial boundaries.

Two preliminaries

A detailed analysis of the present political situation of the Muslim States would need to stress two preliminary questions of great moment for the Arab Near East, on the one hand, and the Maghreb, on the other. The friendship or enmity of the Muslim countries with regard to the Western democracies is at stake in both cases.

In the East there is the painful question of the State of Israel. The Arab countries refused to acknowledge its legitimacy. Their motive is not primarily one of an urge for domination nor of anti-Jewish racialism, as a Western observer might imagine: it is only once the battle has been joined that such instinctive simplifications may come to the surface and predominate. The real motive is to be found in a principle of traditional Muslim law deeply ingrained in the mind of every Muslim, namely, that once a land is part of the *dar al-Islam*, it must never be severed from the Community (*umma*). It was this very motive which, at the time of the Crusades, urged the reconquest of the Frankish Kingdoms of Syria and Palestine in the name of the "Holy War" that lasted for two centuries. At the present day all the Arab countries, whatever their divisions, rally, at least officially and verbally, whenever the Israeli question arises.

This is not the place to propose concrete solutions to this situation, but the gravity of the atmosphere of hatred, constantly maintained, requires to be noted. It is all too easy to succumb to the temptation to foster hatred as a means of ensuring political unity. The problem of Israel could easily shift from politics to racialism—contrary to all the principles of Islam. Then again, the modern economic structure and the advanced technical achievements of Israel give it, in the eyes of the Arabs, the appearance of the forerunner of dreaded imperialism.

Whatever solution may eventually be found, there is an immediate problem on hand, that of the Palestinian Arab refugees who throw themselves on the mercy of the civilized world. It is true that in most Arab countries where they have taken refuge, there has been no attempt to integrate the Palestinians; rather they have been stimulated to aspire to return to their countries. But Israel has refused their readmission without a peace treaty to guarantee her own security. Thus for the past ten years, hostages of rival political powers, some 900,000 refugees—mostly in Jordan—live, summer and winter, in tents or makeshift houses, without means of livelihood, beggars at the door of UNO, waiting for a solution that never comes. Their moral distress is worse than their material conditions. Poverty sought out for the love of God is rewarded with peace; but the crushing yoke of wretchedness spells only death.

In the Maghreb, for years the "Algerian war" has piled up slaughter and enmity. We do not intend to go into the history of this conflict, still less to assess it. All we shall say here is that it is quite certain that the young independent States of Morocco and Tunisia will never be able to play the part of a link between the East and the West to which they aspire, neither will they be able to go forward towards free and genuine friendship with the European countries of the Mediterranean seaboard, as long as Algeria remains in a state of disruption in search of its destiny.

The unity and solidarity of the three countries of the Maghreb is a clear fact. Nothing constructive will be done in any one of them independently of the general interests of all three. The link between any one of them and other nations may be more or less close, but there is undeniable evidence of the interdependence of Tunisia, Algeria and Morocco. The whole of the *dar al-Islam* is by definition a community in sentiment and mutual aid, but here these characteristics are given a tangible embodiment in the historical trends and the geographical and economic condition of these countries.

Tunisia and Morocco are, indeed, deeply imbued with that desire and pride in "living together" which is characteristic of Arab and Arabized peoples in the *umma*. But unlike the leading countries of the Near East they seem disposed within the setting of those basic elements, to welcome the establishment of friendly relations with the Western countries and even the cultural inheritance which these countries retain from their Christian past. On the level of Islam as such, we have seen that Morocco is evolving along the lines of a non-secularizing reform and is showing a quiet self-confidence in the social and economic field. That perhaps may prove to be in the Maghreb the only possible answer to the seductions of Marxism. But such perspectives of the future would certainly be obscured if an effective and just solution were not found to the problems of Algeria. If the natural tendencies of the people of the Maghreb became involved in a jealousy and antagonism towards the West, all the wise and prudent goodwill shown by the governments of Morocco and Tunisia when they attained their independence would run the risk of being swept utterly away. The political and economic endeavours of Morocco and Tunisia would come to nothing if they ignore the realities of the Algerian situation. And perhaps in the train of the Maghreb the destiny of the whole of Africa may be at stake.

MARXISM

It can be said at once that the vision of the Marxist world exercises no attraction on the Muslim, but that the Marxist economy and its efficiency constitute a real seduction for them. Three different fundamental attitudes can be distinguished:

1. We may take first the attitude of the leading figures in the Syro-Egyptian United Republic. There is here no political subservience. The Western press has more than once misrepresented this point. The Syro-Egyptian looked towards the U.S.S.R. (and its satellites) as the only one of the great powers that offered "beneficent" aid. We recall the turn Egyptian politics took at the time of the Suez expedition and of America's refusal to finance the Aswan Dam. America wanted an alliance in exchange for aid; the U.S.S.R. looks only for "positive neutrality". And neutrality, even "positive" neutrality, is the thing that the Near East countries have long since set their hearts on.

Technical, financial and even military aid from the U.S.S.R. are not looked on by the Arab governments as entailing the adoption of the Marxist pattern of life, much less Marxist atheism. They are quite clear in their own minds that that pattern of life is to be rejected. (They are equally clear about rejecting the principles of international capitalism, which for them spells "imperialism".) Indeed they show little interest in adopting the economics of Marxist countries.

They repeatedly assert their readiness to accept capital investments from all countries indifferently, provided that does not diminish their own independence. It must be recognized that the Arab countries still linked economically with the West (thus Arabia and Jordan) only stand apart from Syria and Egypt in this respect because they hope thus to preserve their dynastic privileges.

2. But it may well be that countries such as Arabia, and still more so Jordan, will find that they have to take into account the deep-rooted sentiment of their peoples, who feel a much greater preference for Arab greatness than for alliances with the West. Then again, the Syro-Egyptian rulers (and this may soon be true of Iraq) do not realize to what an extent Soviet aid and propaganda can influence the outlook of their élite.

There are, in fact, very many educated Arabs who are set on maintaining the fundamental values of Islam, above all belief in One God, and at the same time, against this background of monotheism, want to promote the social and economic principles of Marxism. It is here that the slogans of Soviet propaganda find an echo in the spontaneous desires of the people, with their antagonism towards "capitalist imperialism" as productive of the "colonial régime". The more clear-sighted of them, moreover, are aware that most Muslim countries are now classified as underdeveloped, and that they lag far behind the standard of living of Western countries and that they can never catch up if they depend on the means normally provided by a capitalist economic system. It is all too natural that concern for the welfare of their people, and their need of resources to ensure at least a minimum standard of living, should make them look, not only to a planned economy, but to an economy planned by force as in the Marxist countries. In this matter the attraction is not so much the picture of the U.S.S.R. as that of the People's China, that huge Asiatic China which was, like them, swept by Western imperialism—the Bandung mentality once more—and is now busy organizing itself to provide food and clothing for its 600 million inhabitants. It is no rare thing to find young Muslims, reformers or modernists, who have been to China and have come home full of hope.

3. But, to say the least, there is no firm foothold between Marxism taken as an economic system and the pattern of life which that system creates and enforces. There are precious few Muslims who have embraced Marxism to the extent of professing atheism. But there are some. The people, spontaneous in their faith, though often illiterate, do not succumb to Marxism whole and entire. But among the young intelligentsia, who owe their education in the Near East and in the Maghreb to Western culture, Marxism offers ever-present food for thought.

Official optimism in Muslim countries declares that Islam is an insurmountable barrier to atheistic Communism. In reality, such optimism has already been somewhat discountenanced and Islam is seen to be a far less formidable barrier than Western Christianity, even in diaspora. True enough, the spiritual principles of Islam are incompatible with Marxism. But that supposes an Islam lived with deep conviction: and that is in no way encouraged by the failure to revitalize Islamic religious sciences nor by the influence of a secularized West. It is through its technical achievements and its conquests that the secularized West has impressed so many young Muslims. It is for similar reasons that Marxism exercises its attraction, with the added appeal of quicker results. Long before any political pacts were formed, Arabic translations of the works of Marx and Lenin were in great demand in Damascus. Revolutionary Egypt for years forbade the sale of Communist literature. But such an interdiction could scarcely be maintained once a pro-Russian policy had been adopted. And the sudden lifting of the ban made the hitherto forbidden books all the more attractive. It is, of course, only, or almost only, the young people who have been attracted, and even then only a minority. But revolutions have often had their origins in a small minority of intellectuals. It is not only the prospect of a revival in Islam that is at stake, it is the very religious and spiritual atmosphere of Islam as such.

The mass of the people have lost nothing of their faith. But they are deeply moved by anything that bears on the greatness and independence of, not perhaps so much their own particular little country, as the "Arab nation". And it so happens that what they hear on the radio and what they read in their papers is the pro-Arab politics of the U.S.S.R. and the persistent imperialism of the West. Hence they are drawn in the direction which Marxist dialectics foresaw.[1]

It is indeed quite certain that Soviet policy has been and continues to be extremely clear-sighted in regard to the Arab peoples—and that Western policies, sometimes better intentioned than is usually made out, have been and are still remarkably short-sighted. Their greatest weakness is perhaps that they have failed to see the Arab Muslim world in its true historical perspective and deep down this is all too frequently due, there seems no doubt, to ignorance of Islam and of Muslim values.

As a result only too often a paradoxical situation is reached: the Western democracies, who never tire of talking about the dignity of the human person and the common heritage of cultural wealth, are closely tied in the Arab-Muslim countries to the ancient social structure and the feudal chiefs, whose one thought is to use capitalist economics as a means of maintaining their privileged position; at the same time the young "intellectuals", trained in the school of the West, turn hopeful eyes towards the Marxist countries and attack the West with its own arms. In this they may well be logical, turning towards Marxism as to the ultimate conclusion of a secularization which has excluded God from the commonwealth.

It is too early to assess the attempts made in Morocco

[1] The same risk is increasingly run by Muslims in "black" Africa.

where, in the name of Islamic values, Marxism is rejected, even as a temporary political alliance, and efforts are being made to set on foot a universally beneficial collectivist economy, neither capitalist nor communist. May the help and sympathy with which this has met from outside continue to come from Christian sources and thus prove that there are for the Muslim world other means of efficient progress and other planned economic systems besides trusts and historical dialectical materialism.

Marxist theories with their attractive façade hold the attention of those responsible for the economic evolution of the *dar al-Islam* as in all underdeveloped countries. Nevertheless, as the peoples become aware of their needs, it is the problem of social evolution that is the first to be raised.

EDUCATION

Illiteracy weighs heavily on most Muslim countries. It is perhaps only in Syria and the Lebanon that it has been effectively tackled. Throughout the modern age education has progressed in Europe and America. But the Islamic countries, during their long dormant epoch, have remained where they were in the Middle Ages, with an educated and often highly cultured élite and an illiterate populace. Today this is one of their greatest handicaps.

In assessing this situation there is this to be borne in mind. Prior to the technical age everybody benefited by what in practice amounted to an education. It was communicated by a sort of osmosis and was often dissociated from instruction. It was not everyone, unfortunately, who had opportunity for instruction, but what all could obtain was a moral education, and that was perhaps more important. We need only recall certain nomads or peasants in North Africa or the Near East, who have preserved a delicate sense of the virtue of hospitality and mutual help, a profound sense of justice and constancy in their word of honour. Illiterate undoubtedly, but able to recite by heart and even to compose narratives, enigmas, folklore poems replete with wisdom drawn from the people's distant past.

It would most certainly be wrong to suggest that these ancient nomadic and rural groups are without education. But it is clear that they are singularly ill-equipped to meet the invasion of technology. And so they disintegrate and their ancient native wisdom, for all its charm, is soon dethroned. The fact is that this kind of education is confined to what a people remembers of its past. The technical progress of the modern world stresses the necessity for each individual to be adequately equipped to contribute to the development and renovation of his cultural inheritance.

Most of the independent Muslim States have taken up this task with determination. Almost everywhere school facilities have been made free and compulsory. In Egypt this includes secondary education.[2] But in the case of economically under-developed countries, the provision of educational facilities is a slow and difficult business. In Egypt, for instance, the results are already appreciable, whereas in Iraq they still fall short of requirements.

We may here recall once more the efforts made by the Moroccan Government. They soon realized that something more than the typically European style of schooling was needed. Constant efforts are maintained in regard to, firstly, basic education and, secondly, popular education. The most recent techniques and experiments of UNESCO have been called in. One whole winter a campaign was conducted throughout the villages and townships of Morocco. Newspapers, radio, and—something new for the Muslim people—the theatre, are used to interest all classes of people in education. Furthermore—and this is of the greatest

[2] But the pupils are obliged to wear European dress, and this is a real obstacle in poor areas and places where tradition has a strong hold.

importance—there is a determination to provide facilities for further education to follow up the initial stages.

This struggle against illiteracy aims first, in Arab Muslim countries, at teaching Arabic, just as in Turkey it teaches Turkish. And the Arabic is, of necessity, what is known as literary Arabic, which is fundamentally the language of the Koran, though made more flexible to suit modern needs. Some orientalists are of the opinion that the dialects should be the vehicle for future Arab culture and that literary Arabic should be to Islam what Latin is to Christianity. But they are clearly ill-informed and too taken up with the pattern of things in Europe. The Arabic dialects are not written. The radio and the cinema sometimes use them; the young Moroccan theatre, so full of vitality, uses everyday language so as to reach the general public, just as the theatre in Tunisia did even for several years prior to independence. But the trend in basic schooling and popular education is towards classical (literary) Arabic.

But there is a further complication. Once there is a question of secondary education the question of study of a modern European language arises. There are two factors to be considered here. Firstly, during the period when these recent independent states were reawakening to their own individuality, they were either protectorates or, like Turkey and Iran, were pursuing a policy of westernization. The young élite, who did most towards the nationalist movements, thus derived their outlook from foreign sources and it sometimes happened that in some measure they had lost their Arab culture. This is particularly noticeable in the Maghreb. Thus there were Tunisians and Moroccans who, in the long run, came to use French in preference to any other language as the vehicle of culture. This was still more in evidence in Algeria. It is true that this was due to force of circumstances rather than to free choice. But people who grew up in the transitional period are still often bilingual, speaking Arabic and French in the Maghreb, the Lebanon and Syria, Arabic and English or Arabic and French in Egypt, Arabic and English in Iran and Jordan, Hindustani and English in Pakistan. This cultural duality is of its nature transitory. The example of Egypt proves that. At the time of the khedives and the kings, French and Turkish were the languages of the court, though it is true to say now that the Arabization of Egypt is an accomplished fact.

But even after total Arabization, the Islamic countries will still need a second language for technical purposes and international relations. English and French come first and then German and Spanish; and, undoubtedly, present relations with the U.S.S.R. and the large number of bursaries offered by the Universities of Moscow and Leningrad will popularize the study of Russian. Tunisia and Morocco still teach French in the top classes of their primary schools. In Egypt and Iraq advanced science and medicine are taught in English.

While all this brings an added difficulty to the development of education for the illiterate mass of the population, it does hold out certain advantages. It can only lead to impressively greater possibilities for cultural exchange, provided Arabic and its richness of expression become widely studied in Europe and elsewhere; and cultural advance will gain thereby.

EMANCIPATION OF WOMEN

The traditional pattern of Muslim life puts a rigid social barrier between men and women. This is manifested notably in the following ways: seclusion of women, the veiling of the face from marriageable age, early marriage determined arbitrarily by paternal authority (*jabr*) or that of a guardian, polygamy, unilateral and absolute right of the husband to repudiate his wife with very limited rights for the woman to request a divorce, and even then only before a religious court. Within each household the wife or wives had to stay in the harem (*haram*, a sacred and forbidden place), where the only menfolk allowed to enter were near relatives. In the towns the Muslim woman could never leave the house except on rare occasions to go to the cemetery or the baths, or to visit friends, but always accompanied. In poor families, especially in the country, the requirements of work made it practically impossible to observe these customs.

Yet these things were only *customs*. There were Muslim women who played a notable rôle in the beginnings of Islam. In the course of the centuries there have been women poets of renown and there were mothers of sovereigns who played an important political rôle. The Koran, it is true, bids the "wives of the Prophet" and the "wives of believers", to "hold their veils firmly", "in order to remain chaste" (33, 59; 24, 31), but neither the Koran nor the *hadith* commanded Muslim women in general to remain secluded or to hide their faces completely with a veil. There are *hadith*, accepted as authentic, which require mutual consent for marriage and stipulate that cohabitation must not begin before puberty. The Koran permits polygamy and allows four legitimate wives, but it by no means imposes polygamy and, indeed, it lays down conditions for it which can prove difficult to fulfil (Koran, 4, 3). The unilateral right to repudiate is undoubtedly permitted, but it would be more correct to say that it is only tolerated[3] or even that its practice is advised against.

As Muslim countries become more modernized, so the education and emancipation of women becomes more marked. Not always rapidly, perhaps, but irresistibly. There are Muslim women who dress as Europeans. If they belong to well-to-do families, they attend school, college and university, sit for examinations and take up a trade or profes-

[3] The Koran indeed sets out to regulate repudiation and to guarantee the rights of a repudiated woman. The context implies that repudiation is a pre-Islamic custom and that the new legislation seeks to suppress its abuses (Koran, 2, 226–32; 65, 1–6).

sion. They become midwives, doctors, lawyers, journalists, teachers. If they belong to poor families they work away from their homes and, in industrialized areas, find employment in factories. It even happens that, contrary to all usage, the husband is out of work and the wife is the bread-winner. Also, partly for economic reasons and partly in compliance with the new pattern of life, in most secularized or modernized Muslim States, polygamy is only found as a sporadic survival of the past. There are also numerous newspapers and congresses which promote emancipation.

The emancipation of women has naturally been seen by some people as a divorce from the intimate religious character of Muslim life, a kind of secularization. And people who have thus complied with this emancipation may well imagine that they have departed from the prescriptions of Islam as such. But the "orthodox" reformers and leading feminists have not been slow to examine this matter in the light of the tenets of Islam. The considerations listed in the last paragraph about the veil, seclusion, parental authority and polygamy as permissible but not imposed, repudiation as only tolerated, all this has been freely aired in books, newspapers and reviews. The reformists declare that such emancipation is a necessity and, so long as it respects the fundamental rights and duties of woman in the household, it is not only compatible with enlightened Muslim faith but is even demanded by it.[4] And indeed, many "feminists" are sincere and loyal believers.

The developments so far introduced on these lines vary considerably from country to country. The feminist movement, with secularist leanings, has been in evidence in

[4] In his book *al-Nuqd al-dhati* ("Self examination") published in Cairo, 1952, Allal al-Fasi, Moroccan Istiqlal leader, wrote: "The authorization of polygamy is linked with conditions of equality and justice which are practically unrealizable today. What is more, polygamy often provides our adversaries with an argument against our religion itself. All the more reason for suppressing it without delay."

Egypt for a considerable time. The use of the veil has almost disappeared. Sports clubs and even cadet corps are open to women. In the towns, cases of polygamy are few and far between. Repudiation has perforce given way legally to divorce on the Western pattern.

Since Tunisia achieved independence it has forbidden polygamy. The official reasons for this, put forward by President Bourguiba, echo the arguments of the advanced reformists who follow the teaching of Mohammed Abduh and appeal to an interpretation of the Koran adapted to present-day social and economic conditions. Morocco recently drew up a new (Muslim) Legal Code from which the prescriptions introduced by an unenlightened tradition have been eliminated. There also, divorce has taken the place of repudiation and, while the wording of the code does not suppress polygamy, its trend is wholly towards monogamy. Also, a girl is not allowed to marry until after her sixteenth birthday.

The principles of equal civic rights for women and the right of womenfolk to education and social life are everywhere admitted in the new Muslim States. Universal suffrage and entry to many trades and official positions are beginning to be recognized.[5]

The problem now is to prepare the Muslim woman for her new circumstances. But there is a danger that the kind of emancipation adopted may be that of the dechristianized West, with its purely relative moral values, to the detriment of authentic Islam. Here once more is a field in which sincere and disinterested Christian fellowships may have a beneficial influence of considerable importance. It is certain that the human value of the new Muslim States will depend on the kind of contribution Muslim women make to family and public life.

[5] Muslim women have acted as nurses in the fighting in Algeria and have even been combatants. This must surely have a decisive effect on the social evolution of Algerian women.

PROLETARIAT AND SUB-PROLETARIAT

In the traditional Muslim commonwealth the sub-proletariat was unknown. And by sub-proletariat we imply people cut off from the native environment, *déclassés*, or who have never known anything other than indescribable material poverty, living in overcrowded and makeshift dwellings, with only spasmodic work and an ever-present spectre of unemployment. There were, indeed, poor people and beggars in Islamic lands but, in some sort, provision was made for them in the general pattern of life and they were the responsibility of the community. There were apprentices, master craftsmen, small traders, all earning their livelihood, but all sure of work. The tradesmen's property was safeguarded by a corporation, which also concerned itself with salaries and prices.

The only proletariat in the Muslim social pattern were the peasants and farmers with their own or rented farms, toiling from sunrise to sunset and with a very low standard of living. They were often shackled to a wretched plot of land, ever on the verge of debt, undernourished and the victims of famine whenever the harvest failed. Many Egyptian fellahs, among others, still live like that, awaiting the improvements which current agricultural reforms are to bring them. In comparison with the fellahs, who work land which does not belong to them, the nomads, who own their tents and their herds of cattle, are privileged folk. Peasant life has always been looked down on in Islam, while the life of a nomad is thought of as something honourable.[6] Indeed, apart from a few groups living in oases, it was originally a rare thing to find Arab peasants. The peasants of Syria, Iraq and Egypt were at first colonized people, and even after their conversion to Islam, they were still looked on under the Umayyads as

[6] On seeing a ploughshare in the house of one of his Medinan partisans, Mohammed is supposed to have said: "Such things never enter a house without bringing abasement with them." This is a well-known *hadith* quoted by Ibn Khaldun.

enfranchised serfs whose land belonged to the State. They had to pay a special tax called *kharaj*.

Undoubtedly, drought and famine can be disastrous for the nomad and then, if he has no prospects, he gives up the nomadic life. The only thing for him to do is to sell his tent and his goods and chattels and swell the ranks of a sedentary class, who have neither roots nor employment.

The foremost reason for the great importance attached to current agricultural reforms in the majority of Muslim States is that the ancient patriarchal system is an encumbrance to the application of modern industrialized farming and its economic output. And besides this, social economic principles, to be really effective, must operate on a world-wide basis. The under-nourished fellah cannot coexist indefinitely with the farmers of Australia and America. That could only mean that he would be at the mercy of the vicissitudes of the international market and transformed, perhaps, from a member of the proletariat into a member of the sub-proletariat.

But at the present time it is in the modern Muslim towns that the evil of the sub-proletariat is at its worst, pathetically associated with Western influence and recent industrialization. The process is an all too familiar one. On the one hand the population is continually on the increase, thanks to the progress made in hygiene, the suppression of local skirmishes and the care taken to protect human life generally—though nothing has so far been done to ensure that improvements in rural areas keep pace with those in the towns. Along with this there are more and more factories in the towns and harbour installations are being developed. Hence there is a demand for labour, skilled and unskilled. Now this industrialization was launched on the lines of liberal capitalism or trusts and for a long time little if anything was done for the social resettlement of the workers uprooted from their own environment. The surplus population of the rural areas was drawn by the mirage of town life, with its means of livelihood that needed no initial outlay.

Once in the towns, these fellahs or sons of fellahs, accustomed to living in their village hovels, instinctively set about building themselves makeshift dwellings, and thus shanty-towns grew up. Then, with an economic crisis, instead of a demand for labour there was unemployment. Social laws were all too slow in coming and there was still more delay before they could be properly administered. And meantime, in and around the large towns, appalling shanty-towns had come into being, crammed with an impossible density of population—a sub-proletariat living in absolutely sub-human conditions.

This tragic situation is perhaps more in evidence in the Maghreb, where industrialization is more widespread. There are, for example, the shanty-town of Borgel near the port in Tunis, the Glacier district on the outskirts of Algiers and Mahiedinne in the centre of the town and many other districts, among them the Casbah, which was at one time the fashionable Moorish quarter but has now become a refuge for an incredibly overcrowded population. Worst of all, perhaps, is the vast belt of shanty-towns encircling Casablanca. Tunisia and Morocco, now independent, seek to resolve the situation of the shanty-towns, a burdensome legacy from the past.

The problem is far more than one of housing facilities, as Tunisia and Morocco well know: it is a problem of productivity, employment and social education. The advance made towards automation in industry is making the mass of unskilled labour redundant. Industrialization of the towns is indispensable but, if it is to be brought about without doing harm, it must be accompanied by deconcentration of industry and the development of agriculture, for these countries are predominantly rural in character.

Thus the workers in the towns will be enabled to regain their dignity and personality as workers. Wherever Islam has come into contact with modern industrialization, the framework of its traditional corporations has collapsed. It is to be expected that the problems associated with industry will become increasingly acute in Muslim countries and will be more keenly felt there than in Europe, because of the sudden disruption of their ancient closed communities. It is no rare thing to find the Muslims, even women, abruptly transported from their quiet country town to a factory. Gone are the craftsmen's corporations: it is the trade unions that now take over and with them rests, in a large measure, the education of the manual worker.

Soviet Communism took these developments in hand among the Muslims in the U.S.S.R. as early as 1920–2. These were decisive years. Since then, either directly or through the various local Communist parties, the U.S.S.R. has kept up a double campaign, social and political, in other countries. This propaganda has been particularly virulent in Indonesia and Afghanistan and, before the partition, in India also. It keeps a close watch on industrial development and the rise of the proletariats, and if these are not forthcoming it creates them. Iran is a case in point.

But sometimes the trade unions controlled by the U.S.S.R. were outrun by national unions which were stimulated by a simultaneous urge for the betterment of the workers' lot through greater social justice and for the achievement of political independence. The trade unions in Tunisia and Morocco played a decisive rôle in the struggle for independence and they are resolved to do everything in their power towards the development and greatness of their countries. Morocco decided not to have more than one trade union and the U.M.T. (Moroccan Workers' Union) came to an understanding with the Istiqlal trends of the government.

This question of trade unionism arises also in the Near East, though in a less acute form. In Egypt, it is provided for by the authority of the single party. But Egypt's industrial policy and the fact that she is assured of considerable investments from Marxist countries of Eastern Europe will undoubtedly lead the working classes to play a preponderant rôle in politics. But the foremost question for Egypt is still the agricultural proletariat. The programme of the agricultural reform promulgated on September 9th, 1952, has not yet been completed: there are considerable difficulties and the results are far from adequate. In 1956 a third of the land taken from the big landowners by compulsory purchase had still not been allocated. The essential task for Egypt is to ensure the country's economic independence, resolve the rural proletariat and prevent the rise of an urban proletariat. Whatever may happen, it is clear that the population of Egypt is increasing by leaps and bounds. The greatest problem is therefore to guarantee work for all. In view of this, great store is placed on the prospects of new land from the building of the Aswan Dam, the use of the waters of the Nile and on the recruiting of the surplus rural population.

In the field of economic and political independence, the emancipation of women and the family, the resolving of the proletariat, general and social education of the working classes, the Muslim countries stand at the crossroads. The choice is on the one hand between a secularization, which for a time will temporize with individual consciences but deny God any place in public life as such, or, on the other, a new solution derived from the ethos of Islam, but in a purer and more widely embracing formula.

It would seem that the former choice would sooner or later lay these countries open to the bait held out by atheistic dialectical materialism, and no defence could be found in falling back on Arab unity or Arab greatness. It is only in the other choice that there can be hope of a truly human solution and of a dialogue with present-day Christianity, fostering respect for the rights of God and the rights of man and leading to the establishment of a better way of life in this world. But this second choice is also the more clear cut: it enlists the whole man unreservedly and, by the same token, counts on him to realize that he is a creature endowed with intelligence and will but that he has not within himself the ultimate purpose of his existence.

CONCLUSION

This book leaves a great deal still to be said about Islam. Can we, in conclusion, endeavour to discern the specific attitude of Islam?

At the centre of Islam's faith is the inaccessible mystery of One God, at the centre of its moral code is obedience to the divine Words. Morality, considered as leading to the last end, coincides in some sort with faith itself. The moral precepts, exacting though they may be, demand in the first place that man's life should be lived in relation to prescriptions determined by God. That is the reality of faith which, alone and of itself, determines the salvation of man. And faith *is* intrinsically witness. The "good works" that are prescribed—whether moral or social or liturgical—taken together, are the fulfilment, a complement, of faith, but they do not animate faith in its intrinsic vitality. For the "works" themselves are founded on the discontinuous commandments of God.

Islam came to a halt, as it were, on the night of the "ascension" of its Prophet, on the mysterious threshold of the divine Essence, the threshold, therefore, of the mystery of the love of the living God. And when "those that thirst for God", who were the product of Sufism, sought to cross that threshold, the only guide they had was their own interior experience, measured by their response to the graces which God unceasingly offers to all men. The greatest and purest of them, it may be thought, lived out in their lives the vital link of faith with love; they discovered that suffering accepted and loved was the way of love. In the words of Hallaj: "All things necessary to me, them indeed have I received, except him who would cause my ecstasy to exult in the depths of anguish."

Faith, and salvation which depends on it, as well as retribution for human acts, have primarily in Islam an eminently personal character. It is each man, separately, who will be judged in the day of the Assembling. "No burdened soul shall bear the burdens of another; nothing shall be reckoned to a man but that which he has accomplished."[1]

But it is the *umma*, the Community as such, which bears witness to God, and it is at the community and temporal level that the prescription to "command the good" is seen in its quintessence.

Now there is a well-known tradition which says that the faith of the Community will become gradually degraded in the course of ages until, at a determined time, when impiety is rife, the omnipotent justice of God will be manifested by the annihilation of creatures, their resurrection and their judgement. That is the hour, eschatologically imminent, when man will give an account of himself. This hour will be preceded by the coming of the Mahdi, the supreme guide, the awaited, the desired of believers. The texts, and the Koran itself, portray the day of the last judgement as reserved by God to himself alone, surrounded undoubtedly by assessors, but he the one Judge in his transcendence. In the preliminaries of the judgement, tradition came to declare that Mohammed would intercede for the sinful believer of his Community, and they maintain that Jesus, "whose name is Messiah", will return. More than this, it is sometimes said that "Jesus the Son of Mary", "the Word (come) from God" ... "in the womb of Mary" and "fortified by the Spirit of sanctity",[2] will be commissioned by God to preside over the great court of the Assembly. Other texts assign this rôle to Mohammed or to Ali or to a descendant of the "people of the House". Here again, Islam comes to the threshold of divine life and there halts at the "Sidrah tree which marks

[1] Koran, 53, 38–9.
[2] *Ibid.*, 3, 45.

the boundary",[3] beyond which the mystery revealed would make it possible to grasp the Absolute of the precept of love and therefore the absolute of the human act in relation to eternity.

Faced with the question relentlessly put before the faith of Islam by "those that thirst for God", the "pious believers" bear witness to faith in God the Most High, who speaks to men through his prophets and envoys, only revealing his "wondrous Names" by which he designates himself—a veil behind which he remains concealed. Abraham is the friend of God, Moses his interlocutor, Jesus his Word and Mohammed the Seal of his prophets. God has made provision for his servants in this world and the next. The interior attitude of the "believer" (*mumin*) is a total confident surrender in darkness to God, who is not to be questioned but who is known to be the just Judge, the Help and the Surety.

[3] *Ibid.*, 53, 14.

SELECT BIBLIOGRAPHY

ARBERRY, A. J.: *Avicenna on Theology* (selections from his works), London, John Murray, and Hollywood-by-the-Sea, Fla, Transatlantic Press, 1951; *Sufism*, London, Unwin, and New York, Macmillan, 1956; *The Legacy of Persia*, London and New York, Oxford Univ. Press, 1953; *Moorish Poetry*, Cambridge and New York, Cambridge Univ. Press, 1953; *Ibn Hazm: The Ring of the Dove*, London, Luzaq, 1953.

ARNOLD, Th., and GUILLAUME, A.: *The Legacy of Islam*, London and New York, Oxford Univ. Press, 1931.

BABOUR, Nevil: *A Survey of North West Africa* (the Maghreb), London and New York, Oxford Univ. Press, 1959.

BAILLIE, Neil B. E.: *A Digest of Muhammadan Law*, Lahore, 1958.

BECKINGHAM, C. F.: *Atlas of the Arab World and the Middle East*, London, Macmillan, and New York, St Martin's Press, 1960.

BLOCHET, E.: *Muslim Painting*, London, Methuen, 1929.

BONNÉ, Alfred: *Economic Development of the Middle East*, London, Kegan Paul, and New York, Humanities Press, 1953.

BROCKELMAN, Carl: *History of the Islamic Peoples*, London, Kegan Paul, and New York, Putnam, 1959.

DANIEL, Norman: *Islam and the West*, Edinburgh, University Press, and Chicago, Quadrangle Books, 1960.

DIMAND, M. S.: *A Handbook of Muhammadan Art*, New York, Metropolitan Museum of Art, 1958.

FRYE, Richard N. (Editor): *Islam and the West* (Papers read at the Harvard Summer School on the Middle East), The Hague, Mouton, and New York, Lounz, 1955.

GIBB, H. A. R.: *Modern Trends in Islam*, Chicago, Univ. of Chicago Press; (Editor) *Ibn Battuta*, London, Kegan Paul, 1957.

GIBB, H. A. R., and BOWEN, Harold: *Islamic Society and the West*, London and New York, Oxford Univ. Press, 1957.

GIBB, H. A. R., and KAMERS, J. H.: *A Shorter Encyclopaedia of Islam*, Leiden, J. Brill, 1953, and Ithaca, N.Y., Cornell Univ. Press, 1957.

GRUNENBAUM, G. E. von: *Unity and Variety in Muslim Civilization*, Chicago, Univ. of Chicago Press, 1955; *Muhammadan Festivals*, London and New York, Abelard-Schuman, 1958.

GUILLAUME, A.: *Life of Muhammad*, London and New York, Oxford Univ. Press, 1955.

HAZARD, H. W., and COOKE, H. L.: *Atlas of Islamic History*, Princeton, N.J., Princeton Univ. Press, 1954.

The Koran: translated by George Sale, London and New York, Fredk Warne, various edns; translated by J. M. Rodwell, London, Dent, and New York, Dutton, 1909 (several reprints).

LANDAU, Rom: *Islam and the Arabs*, London, Unwin, 1958; *The Philosophy of Ibn Arabi*, London, Unwin, 1959.

LAQUEUR, Walter Z.: *Communism and Nationalism in the Middle East*, London, Kegan Paul, and New York, Praeger, 1957.

LEWIS, B.: *The Arabs in History*, London, Hutchinson, and New York, Rinehart, 1950.

NICHOLSON, Reynold A.: *A Literary History of the Arabs*, Cambridge and New York, Cambridge Univ. Press, 1956.

RONART, Stephen and Nandy: *Concise Encyclopaedia of Arabic Civilization*, Amsterdam, Djambatan, 1959.

SMITH, Wilfrid C.: *Islam in Modern History*, Princeton, N.J., Princeton Univ. Press, 1957.

SPULER, Bertold: *The Muslim World*, two volumes, Leiden, J. Brill, 1960.